CW00432222

Pim Kroon

The price of Proximity

LAP LAMBERT Academic Publishing

Imprint

Any brand names and product names mentioned in this book are subject to trademark, brand or patent protection and are trademarks or registered trademarks of their respective holders. The use of brand names, product names, common names, trade names, product descriptions etc. even without a particular marking in this work is in no way to be construed to mean that such names may be regarded as unrestricted in respect of trademark and brand protection legislation and could thus be used by anyone.

Cover image: www.ingimage.com

Publisher:
LAP LAMBERT Academic Publishing
is a trademark of
International Book Market Service Ltd., member of OmniScriptum Publishing Group
17 Meldrum Street, Beau Bassin 71504, Mauritius

Printed at: see last page
ISBN: 978-613-9-44916-3

THE PRICE OF PROXIMITY

An analysis of the willingness to pay of office users for railway station proximity.

Abstract   This research aims to identify the hedonic pricing method for companies in regard to the willingness to pay for their office location nearby a railway station. The goal is to investigate the economic interests by companies and their location choices in relation with the distance to a railway station. The scope of this research is within the Randstad, the Netherlands. This research will be structured by qualitative and quantitative analyses and the insights could be used by local authorities to improve zoning plans in relation to office and railway locations and for investors to provide insight in the hedonic pricing method used by companies in regard to the distance between an office and the nearest railway station and vice versa.

Colofon

Date	: September 2018
Version	: Definitely
Name	: Pim Kroon
Student number	: 5665876
Contact	: kroonpim@gmail.com
University	: University Utrecht
Faculty	: Geoscience
Master	: Spatial Planning
Professor	: Prof. dr. E. (Edwin) Buitelaar
University	: Utrecht University
	Domplein 29
	3512 JE Utrecht

Universiteit Utrecht

Preface

In the summer of 2014 I finished my first study, real estate science, at the Rotterdam University of Applied Sciences. Instead of becoming a real estate agent I wanted to focus on developing real estate. To reach this goal, in 2015 I started my second study, Spatial Planning at the University of Utrecht to extend my skills and knowledge. This study educated me the multiple interests of all actors which are involved in several real estate processes.

In the beginning of this study, I had a job interview for the function 'work student' at JLL, one of the largest real estate consultants in the world. During my study I had the opportunity to work fulltime and developed myself at JLL. Next to the theoretical background in class, I learned the practical lessons in real life concerning real estate transactions. I studied in my own time in the evening and before or after college I was at the office again.
In other words, I had a fulltime job and a fulltime study at the same time and therefore I learned a lot. This results in underlying research, whereby theory is controlled by practice.

Currently, 4 years after I have finished my first study, I haven't developed a single building and I am a professional real estate agent in offices, however I am closer to achieve my goal.

I would like to take the opportunity to thank professor dr. E. Buitelaar for his accompaniment, critics and feedback. Without his advice this research was probably hard, whether impossible, to complete.

Pim Kroon
Rotterdam, September 2018

Summary

'Location, location, location' is what it is all about in the real estate sector. Therefore, it is interesting to investigate what kind of characteristics influences the location with regards to the rent level of an office. The term location has a lot in common with the term proximity. When the proximity is considered as good, will this somehow be expressed in the rent level of an office building. This statement results in the following central question:

"To what extent does the proximity of a railway station affect the rent of office space?"

The analyze starts with a theoretical framework, whereby traditional location theories where used and the railway station is considered as the central point. The expectation is that an office that is located close by a railway station has a higher rent level per square meter lettable floor area than an office that is located further away from a railway station, whereby other relevant characteristics are taken into consideration. This statement is in underlying research investigated.
Conducted by the literature is it clear that not only the distance to the nearest railway station has influence on the rent level of an office, the quality of a railway station, expressed in the RSQI has probably influence as well. Therefore, it is plausible that the RSQI positively moderates the effect of distance on the rent level per sq. m. LFA of an office.
On top of those two hypotheses is a third hypothesis developed that suggests that in a high density and span office market is the effect of distance and the RSQI on the rent level of an office higher than in a less span office market.

The three hypotheses are tested during the execution of a hedonic pricing method. In a hedonic pricing method the consumption is considered as a cohesion of multiple variables that form together the price of a product. The variables are tested using a multiple regression, whereby every characteristic individually can be analysed on their value, as well on their interest that determine the total price of the consumption. In a multiple regression is the relation between the dependent and multiple independent variables calculated. The dependent variable in this research is the rent level per sq. m. LFA of an office and the independent variables are characteristics that theoretically do have influence on the rent level of an office. The proximity to the nearest railway station is the most important independent variable and is defined as distance in meters. The information in the database is provided by multiple sources and are related to office transactions in the years 2013-2017 in the demographic area of the Randstad, the Netherlands. The database consists of 2,940 office transactions in total.

The results of this research show that the variable distance up and including 700 meters from a railway station has significant influence on the rent level per sq. m. LFA of an office. However, in this analysis the RSQI is not included. When the RSQI is included in the hedonic pricing model the results of distance are not significant anymore. Therefore, it can be concluded that the variable RSQI positively moderates the effect of distance on the rent level of an office per sq. m. LFA. and thus is the RSQI more robust than the variable distance.
On top of that, office users in high density and span office markets are less critical on the characteristics of their leased office space and also less critical on the quality of the railway station in comparison with office users is a less span office market.

Finally, this research provides interesting insights in the construction of the rent level of an office and affords governmental and commercial actors an extra support by the decisions in their real estate choices.

Content

Chapter 1   Problem definition

1.1   Background and motivation

The office market in the Netherlands is in an upcoming flow. As the financial crisis passes behind us and the demand for different types of offices at various locations is increasing. The demand is high for offices located near railway stations. Many new offices developments have taken place within railway station locations, over the past few years (NVM, 2017). One of the major causes for these developments is that the market situation can be described as a seller's market, displaying high rents for office buildings near railway stations. Investors or office landlords are able to ask high rents since this segment is in high demand (Jones Lang LaSalle, 2017; Rabobank; 2017). Railway stations obtain for accessibility and accessibility obtain for higher rent levels of offices (Dunning & Norman, 1987; Willigers, Floor & Van Wee, 2007; De Graaff, Debrezion & Rietveld, 2007). But how does the distance and accessibility, by feet, to and from a railway station, influence the rent levels of an office?

During the years, there has been qualitative literature written regarding the effect of accessibility on the success and ancillary rent level of offices. Accessibility is a major driver that will always return in all kind of studies. Because accessibility affects and interpreted the property value in two different ways. First of all, there is physical accessibility, which refers to private or public transportations. Secondly, there is the accessibility of jobs in the direct environment and the accessibility of facilities (Braam, 2014). Literature suggests that accessibility is mostly given as a dichotomy aspect, the accessibility of a railway station is satisfied or it is not. Weterings et. al. (2009) goes further to argue that the quality of a railway station is based on the frequency and the quality of railway traffic to access other stations, which is more important than only the presence of a railway station. Thus, the availability and accessibility of a railway station is not the only sufficient aspect for an office location, but its quality matters as well. As mentioned, does several researchers agree with the fact that accessibility influence the rent level of an office. However, few research is done with regards to the quantitative measurement of the effect of accessibility on the rent level of an office.

The demand for offices is rising and the office location is important for attracting knowledge and talent, (Willigers & Van Wee, 2011; Jones Lang LaSalle, 2017; Leszcynska & Pruchnicki, 2017). Due to the increasing dynamic in mobility and accessibility over the past years (Geurs, 2014; Krabbenborg & Daalhuizen, 2016), the accessibility from and to a railway station may be more important than ever before. An increasing importance of accessibility must have influence on the willingness of organizations to pay for their office location, but the scientific literature does not provide a sufficient answer to this question.

There are three gaps in the literature with regards to this research topic. First of all, the time period of earlier research. The most decent literature of the office values and their accessibility is done by De Graaff, Debrezion and Rietveld, however this research already dates back to 2007. Therefore, it is interesting to analyse whether the rent level of offices nearby railway stations has changed over time as well. On top of that, this research focuses on the Netherlands, with a deep focus on the Randstad. Something which is not investigated before. Third and last gap is that research which is done with regards to the accessibility of a railway station and commercial real estate, is about dwellings or the land value itself and not about office values. Thus, the scientific literature is underexposed so far, especially in relation with quantitative research. Therefore, it is relevant to investigate the relation between a Dutch railway station in the Randstad and the rent level of an office in the direct environment in a quantitative way.

To define the relation between the willingness to pay for an office (location) in relation with the distance from and to a railway station a hedonic pricing method is the most appropriate method. The hedonic pricing method is an economic valuation method, whereby different factors that influence the price of a product are estimated. In this research, the factor will be 'distance from and to a railway station' and 'rent level of an office' will be the price of the product. Due to this method, the results of this research will be measurable and will give an explanation of how the distance and accessibility from and to a railway station influence the rent level of an office.

Since office real estate has the interest of end users and owners, it is of great importance for both parties to know what the financial relation is between the distance of an office to a railway station and the rent level of an office. The research purpose of this thesis is to map and model the relation between the distance from and to a railway station in relation with the rent level of an office(location). Due to this research, a contribution can be made for organizations and office owners, who will make (re)location decisions.

1.2   Research question

Long-term globalization, demographic, policy, cultural, social and economic trends have a major impact on the built environment and underlying real estate market over time. Relocation of an office is a significant event in the life history of any company (Gregory, Lombard & Seifert, 2005) and accessibility of an office is one of the key elements for companies to (re)locate themselves at a specific location. Therefore, accessibility is one of the most important factors that influences the rent level of an office. However, in what way does the distance of an office to a railway station influence the rent level of an office? This leads to the following research question:

"To what extent does the proximity of a railway station affect the rent of office space?"

This research question can be set out in three distinct concepts, namely proximity, rent and office space. The most important aspect to define is the term 'rent'. Within the context of this research I will refer to the rent level which is paid per sq. m. LFA (without incentives and VAT). These prices do not include service charges and/or VAT. The value or price and thus the rent level of a commercial property is based on several factors. Remøy (2010) argues that the three most important factors are namely the market, the location and the building that impact the value or price of a property. In other terms, I will suggest to narrow down the features that influence the value of a property from macro through meso to micro level. The second concept to notice is the term 'proximity'. Proximity cannot be entangled with accessibility. In the literature, proximity is related to the location of the built environment and facilities, whereas accessibility is more related to the connection with public transport and contains an important component: time (Hillbers & Snellen, 2009). The easiest way to make a distinction between these two terms is with an example to describe the proximity and accessibility of the beach. If hotel number one has the description 'located next to the beach' and the second hotel has the description 'beach within a walking distance of 500 meters', the first hotel sounds closer to the beach than the second one. However, if there is a railway with a large fence between hotel number one and the beach, the beach is not accessible at all. In order to reach the beach there is a rail crossing 600 meters away from the hotel. Therefore, hotel number one is further away from the beach than hotel number two, even when the proximity is closer. Thus, in other words: proximity is necessary otherwise you are not accessible, however proximity alone is not enough to be good accessible. Two places with equal proximity to a railway station can have different accessibilities. This research will investigate the influence of the proximity of a railway station in relation to the rent level of an office. Despite the fact that the term accessibility is used in the central question, will this research mostly use the term accessibility. At last, the final concept is the term office space, which can be best described as an area where companies or entrepreneurs are active in producing or providing of goods and merits.

Each concept in this research will focus on testing the influence of the proximity of a railway station in with regards to an office and the willingness to pay more or less if the distance from and to a railway station decreases or increases. This brings focus to this research and results in a correlation whereby the (potential) regression will be revealed. A more detailed explanation about these three subjects will be described in the chapter 2.

1.3   Relevance

1.3.1   Academic relevance

To the best of our knowledge, there is no empirical research done that investigates whether the proximity of Dutch railway stations in the Randstad has provable influence on the value of an office. However, researchers argue that there is an effect on the distance from and to a railway station in relation with the value of a property (Weterings et. al., 2009; De Graaff, Debrezion & Rietveld, 2007; Enström & Netzell, 2008), however this is mostly related to the price of residential housing or land value prices and is not related to the rent level of an office. Furthermore, the interests in mobility have changed significantly over the past years and the financial crisis and many other (accommodation) trends took place. Therefore, it is also interesting to analyse whether the rent level of an office nearby a railway station has changed in comparison with ten years ago. A third and final gap in the academic literature is the lack of focus on the Randstad, the Netherlands. This area is the financial heart of the Netherlands. It is of vital importance to complete the missing academic part as described above. This is mainly due to the fact that (international) research, which measures the direct influence of a railway station on the financial property value of an office, is scarce.

One of the most relevant researches that measures the impact of a railway station on the commercial property value is done by Debrezion, Pels and Rietveld (2007). Their empirical model is based on 73 underlying studies and 57 observations. Although the fact that his research is a meta-study, it is unclear to which city/cities these results are related to. However, they argue that the coefficients for heavy and commuter rail transit are positive, indicating that the effect of heavy and commuter rail transit on property value is greater than light rail transit. They conclude that commuter rail transit stations have a significantly higher effect on property values compared to light rail transit stations. Thus, in conclusion, it can be assumed that larger railway stations, such as intercity stations, do have a positive influence on the value of an office. Nonetheless, it is still unclear how much influence or effect railway stations have on the rent level of an office in the Randstad area. Therefore, it is interesting to investigate the correlation between these variables.

Later on is research by De Graaff, Debrezion and Rietveld (2007) is much more specific. They argue that the distance between a Dutch railway station to an office is of importance in relation to the value of an office and that tenants greatly appreciate the accessibility of a railway station, but do not argue about the willingness to pay for these office locations. In addition, they do not have a geographical focus on the Randstad and the date of research is already deprecated. Last but not least, this research talks about accessibility and does not make the essential distinction with proximity. The results in this research are found by conducting a hedonic pricing method divided over four forms of accessibility: by railway, by road, the distance to Schiphol Airport and the proximity of other offices. The accessibility by rail is indicated with a 'rail station quality index' and within this research all Dutch NS intercity stations are taken into account. Although, this research is relevant and well sourced, there is still a lack of academic relevance with regards to the present time, the demarcation of the Randstad and the explicit result of the affected size of a railway station in relation with the rent level of an office.

1.3.2 Social relevance

The social relevance of this research is significant. As stated by several academic studies and pragmatic research, the demography in the Netherlands is changing. Due to globalization and urbanization, cities are expanding and the periphery is shrinking. The last decades, some regions in the Netherlands have been experiencing population decline (Haartsen & Venhorst, 2010). Dutch planners and policymakers feel the need to develop several strategies for shrinking areas. This has effects in many different ways, such as the departure of organizations and the growing vacancy rates - not only dwellings, but to retail and offices in the outskirts as well. On the contrary, there are also planners who have to think creatively to manage the growth in areas where they barely can handle the growth. This research attempts to identify the effect of offices nearby train stations and the willingness to pay for these locations. As a result, this research contributes to the knowledge to the location theory and whether offices are (still) attractive for companies or not in the direct vicinity of a train station. This research also raises the question in which way the proximity of a train station with regards to an office location is of influence for the attractiveness of tenants.

More insight in these conditions is also beneficial for real estate investors and developers, since it offers them an opportunity to anticipate on the demand of office space and the additional wishes of end users. It would help both better to evaluate the economic potential of assets. Now these evaluations are often based on formulas derived from key conditions similar to those used in new developments. Although these conditions offer useful information, they risk overgeneralization and do not respond to the unique situation of the willingness to pay for office features.

By focusing specifically on the Randstad, the practical relevance of this research becomes more useful for actors in this area. Both governmental actors and commercial actors can benefit from this research. Planning experts and policymakers will benefit from this research by having more insight in future circumstances of office features. This makes it possible to develop their plans and policies less reactive and more proactive. Commercial actors, such as real estate owners, developers and investors, will also benefit from the predictive outcomes of this research. Gaining insight in the future needs for their assets will help them create more effective investment strategies and benefit their evaluation when acquiring new assets.

1.3.3 Demarcation

To fulfil this research within the right borders and to focus on the research purpose, a demarcation has to take place. In the introduction and relevance of the previous sections stands out that research so far is insufficient regarding to find the effect size between the distance to a railway station and the rent level per sq. m. of an office. The real estate office market includes different sectors and stakeholders, such as end users, investors and developers (Van Zon, Van den Berg & De Bue, 2014), whereby different hedonic pricing methods are possible. This research focuses only on office real estate. Therefore, other forms of real estate are not included. The main reason to focus on office real estate in particular, is due to the fact that this market is underexposed in the academic literature so far.

Furthermore, the demarcation of a railway station is important. When the term railway station or train station in this thesis is mentioned, it includes NS stations in the Randstad. The NS is the official Dutch railway provider and is in ownership of the Dutch government.

As mentioned before, this research has a geographical focus on the Randstad area in the Netherlands. Causes to focus on this specific geographical area are outlined below. Firstly, is the popularity of this area: approximately 7 million people live within this area and therefore it does have the highest density in the Netherlands. Secondly, it is also the financial heart of the Netherlands. The total number employments growth is the highest in comparison with other areas in the Netherlands. This means that the Randstad is also a popular area to work. This is shown in the total stock of offices: more than 50% is located in the province of Zuid-Holland and Noord-Holland (PBL, 2017). With the Randstad as demarcation, this thesis will include the four biggest railway stations of the Netherlands as well: Amsterdam, Utrecht, Rotterdam and The Hague. Therefore, a good comparison with smaller railway stations in the Randstad can be made. The geographical demarcation of the Randstad consist of several corop (translated: the coordination commission regional research programmer) regions and includes the agglomerations of 's-Gravenhage, Haarlem and Leiden & Bollenstreek, as well Delft & Westland, Flevoland (Almere), Groot-Amsterdam, Groot-Rijnmond, Het Gooi en Vechtstreek, Oost-Zuid-Holland, Utrecht, Zaanstreek and Zuidoost-Zuid-Holland.

Due to the fact that the one of the gaps in the literature is about the time period, therefore this research focuses on the years between 2013-2017. The latest most relevant research (by De Graaff, Debrezion & Rietveld) dates from 2007 and raises questions whether the results are equal over time. This is interesting particularly because since then, a major development took place over the years with regards to the trends and developments in the real estate office market during a period when the financial crisis took place as well.

Finally, it is important to define the level of abstraction. The purpose of this research, in combination with the research strategy, explains this level of abstraction. The existing relation between distance from or to a Dutch railway station and the rent level or value of an office in the direct environment has to be clear. This thesis aims to explain the relation between both the distance and rent level. In addition, this research aims to compare the results of different intercity stations. Currently, where the scientific research is insufficient about the relation between Dutch railway stations and the rent level of the surrounding offices, it is more relevant to investigate the possible correlation, than to provide an explanation.

1.4   Reading guide

This research is bravely built up in two parts. The first part of this research consists of a theoretical framework and is constructed in chapter 2. By analysing among other things the location theory and rent level characteristics, it is possible to develop a conceptual model whereby the theoretical relations are visualized. Besides the theoretical research, are multiple empirical researches analysed that are published by academic researchers. In chapter 3 is the theory converted into the methodology and is the research method, including the operationalization, discussed and explained.
The second part start in chapter 4 and shows on behalf of a case-study the results of the relation between the distance to the nearest railway station and the rent level of an office building.
This research will end with the conclusion and discussion.

The figure on the right visualize the reading guide.

Chapter 2   Theoretical Framework

The relation whether the proximity of a Dutch railway station has provable influence on the value of an office is not investigated before. In addition, international empirical research that provides insights whether the proximity of a railway station has influence on the value of an office is extraordinary scarce. In order to obtain better insights in this research topic and to expand the current knowledge about this subject is, based on the existing literature and similar topics, a theoretical framework required. In this chapter the existing relations, which are proved by other researchers, will be explained in a qualitative way. To explain and define these relations and correlations, the foundation of this research is laid.

This chapter consists of several subjects and is bravely built up in multiple sections, whereby the theory is most detailed in the last sections. Firstly, the real estate market will be explained by the system of Geltner. The second part consists of office and location features, which are important for the success of real estate. The third section is an explanation of railway stations and the definition of its quality. The term railway station is of high importance for this research and deserves an explicit explanation. After this theoretical and more general part, earlier empirical studies will be discussed. This chapter will end by conducting the theory into a conceptual model.

2.1   The real estate market

This research focuses on the relation between the distance from and to a railway station and the office value. Before an explanation can be given, a short description of the real estate marked will be presented.

The real estate market consists of four different markets: Space Market (rent), Asset Market, Development Industry and Space Market (stock). All these categories have different assumptions with regards to real estate (Geltner et. al., 2014). A clear distinction between the relations helps to expose specific relations, which are relevant in the sequel of this research. Geltner et. al. (2014) explain a model that shows the most important relations in the current commercial real estate market, see figure 1 and relates the four markets with each other. Within the Space Market, there is interaction between the users demand with the current stock of physical space supply and the supply side of landlord who offer office space. The balance between both determines the current rents and occupancy levels in the Space Market. In other words, the take-up and the occupancy rate of commercial real estate depends on supply and demand. Geltner et. al. (2014) explain further that the underlying demand side of the Space Market are the Local & National economies, which determine the need for certain quantities of physical space of various types as a function of the cost (rent) for such space.

The supply and demand of office space determine the shortage of the market. For instance, when demand outweighs supply on the market, shortage appears. Therefore, the occupancy rate will be high and there will be less vacant office space. As a result that the rent levels for offices will increase. This phenomenon works reversed way since less demand and a lot of supply results in lower rent levels.

The demand of office space depends on several factors and trends. These factors and trends depends not only of national economies, but also of local economies (Geltner et. al., 2014). Due to the fact that these factors and trends are various per location, the demand of commercial real estate differs per location. For a long time the real estate maxim 'location, location and location' was the adage in the real estate market as well (Kok, Koponen, & Martínez-Barbosa, 2017) and therefore is the term location one of the most important factors in the commercial real estate market.

Figure 1: The Real Estate System

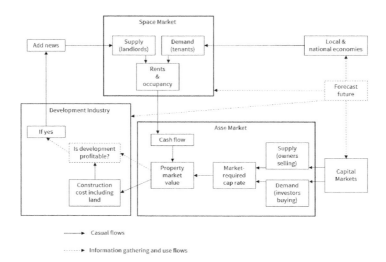

Source: Geltner et. al. (2014)

2.1.1 Office and office location

The commercial real estate market is explained in this model, however a clear distinction between the term office and office location has not been made yet. Both terms are included in the daily procedure of many people and partly because of this, it is hard to define these terms by one clear and central understanding or demarcation. Nonetheless, Buitelaar et. al. (2017) cite Rudolf Bak and define an office as follows: 'a spatial independent unit that is largely in use for desk related activities that are essential for work'. To create a more comprehensive view on this definition, Bijl (2009) describes an office as follows, 'a physical work environment for organizations'. Whether these definitions are combined, the definition of an office in this research will be:

'a physical independent work environment which is largely in use for desk related activities that are essential for work'

One of the characteristics as described by Bijl (2009) is the work environment and related to the interior of an office. However, work environment can also be related to the exterior of an office, the location. An office location is a fuzzy term, but can be related to the clustering of multiple organizations, which are concentrated within a geographical area or to the address of an office building (Van Zon, Van den Berg & De Bue, 2014). In this research is chosen for the address of an office building as the office location. Section 2.2.2 provides more insights about the office location and the interests of this definition.

2.2 Office and location features

The rent level of an office depends on four characteristics: characteristics of the tenant and the lease agreement, characteristics of the property, characteristics of the location and the market circumstances (Weterings et. al., 2009). Within the market circumstances, the demand side has presumably most influence, whether there is more demand than supply, the supply will increase as soon as possible by the construction of new offices for instance. However, this phenomenon does not work reversed way. Therefore, when the demand to real estate decreases, vacant offices are the result. The demand side consists of the total number of end users, such as companies and the investor market. Remøy (2010) suggests that the demand and success of real estate will be characterized based on three different kind of aspects: the market, the location and the building. In this section all three aspects will be explained through different researches.

2.2.1 The market

According to the literature, the commercial office market can best be described as follows: 'In the commercial office markets will office space be sold and bought, and let and rented.' These four forms are always characterized by the demand and supply of office space. Even though the real estate market will barely be on an equal level since there will always be demand for office space at one specific location and always be supply at other locations. The success of the commercial real estate market depends on the demand of office space in relation with the total supply.

Companies and organizations base their accommodation strategies on the expected future demand of their own office space, compared to their supply. By determining the future match between the current demand and supply, a plan of the total needed number of office space in square meters and at which location can be drawn (Remøy, 2010). Despite the easy sound of this theory, it is incredibly difficult to control the real estate (office) market, due to the fact that real estate is immobile and expensive (Gotham, 2006). Geltner et al. (2004) agree and add that it takes much more time to develop offices (real estate in general) than other goods.

Most offices within the uptake of the commercial real estate market are rental offices and approximate 72% of all Dutch office transactions in 2016 took place within the Randstad (Jones Lang LaSalle, 2017). This geographical area is by far the most popular office location in the Netherlands. Paragraph 2.2.2 will discuss the aspect location.

2.2.2 The location

The location, or geographical area, is the most important factor of real estate (Barkham, Bokhari, & Saiz, 2018; Risselada, Schutjens, & Van Oort, 2013). Clapp (1993) argued that the location choice of organizations depends on several factors, which arises from economic theories. One of these economic theories is to locate themselves at a specific location, where the company has most benefits of the direct vicinity in relation with the transportation costs.

Not only the location (address) differ per geographical position, although the economic situation, the trends and other social and cultural influences are different, due to this consists every location over a unique combination of characteristics (Van Zon, Van den Berg & De Bue, 2014). All of these characteristics together forms the popularity of the location. The popularity of a location structure the price, labour costs and the level of tax. According to Clapp (1993) these characteristics are higher in inner cities, where the density is relatively high, in contrast with periphery areas, where the density is low.

In all markets are the economy and trends determinatives for the success of a product, hence in real estate as well. Van Zon, Van den Berg & De Bue (2014) quote several authors and argue that a distinction between the influence on macro- and microeconomic levels. Macroeconomic influences and trends are factors which do have influence in global, continental or national level. And microeconomic influences and trends are factors which do have influence on regional and local level. As a result of the fact that real estate is immobile, the microeconomic factors of the location are more important than it is for other products. In other words, the different economic situations and trends per location partly determine the success of commercial real estate.

The most established location theory is written by Von Thünen (1983 – 1850). Von Thünen gave a predictive model of rural development around an idealized isolated urban center. Imposing several simplifications in an attempt to focus on some of the fundamental processes at work in settlement patterns and rural economic activities (Sasaki & Box, 2003). The theory by Von Thünen emphasizes that this finding can be considered as a generalization towards discovering laws, which govern agricultural prices and translate them into land use patterns. In this land use patterns is the approach considered in terms of the global properties of a city and the surrounding areas. This theory argues that whether more stakeholders will make use of a specific area, the land in that area will be scarce. Scarcity will have influence on the land value and therefore is the central core (where the demand is high) more expensive than places which are located further away from the city center (where the demand is less). Alonso (1964) agrees with this theory and redefines this line of reasoning into a bid-rent model, see figure 2. The idea behind this model is that every person is prepared to pay a certain amount of money, depending on the location of the land or property. This results in a rent slope that declines with distance from the central business district. Figure 2 shows the rent theory of how much different sectors within the economy are prepared to pay for land. The basic assumption is that accessibility is increased with centrality and therefore some kind of retailers, office users, residents and other stakeholders with interests in the city center are prepared to pay a high price for this location. Whether the distance from the city center increases, the availability of land will increases as well. As a result that this type of land is much more affordable for residential and agricultural use, see line III in the figure.

Figure 2: Bid Rent Theory

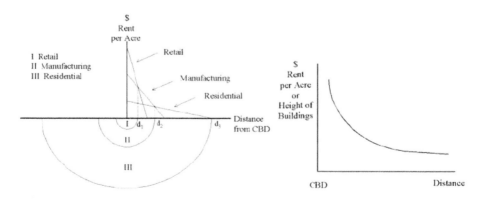

Source: Alonso (1964) – Edited by author

The popularity of a location, district, area or city depends on multiple conditions. Van Zon, Van den Berg & De Bue (2014) quote Miller & Geltner (2005) and sum up the most important factors of growth with regards to the city population. One of these factors is the accessibility of an office building or area. In the literature is accessibility mostly given as a binary aspect: the accessibility is satisfied or it is not. However, there are are two forms of accessibility. The first one is physical accessibility, which is in relation with the means of transportation. Such as private or public transport by road, shipping, aviation a rail. The second form is the accessibility of labour opportunities in the direct environment and the accessibility of other facilities (Braam, 2014). In general, this factor will positively be influenced by the presence of large political and governmental functions and financial services. Additionally, political factors and amenities with regards to the liveability are also important factors for the success of a location.

According to Clapp (1993), organizations are willing to locate themselves at locations where the density of information is high. In other words, in inner cities and especially in the city center. Research by De Graaff, Debrezion & Rietveld (2007) complement that the price of real estate does not only depend on the distance to facilities, but the price also depends on the attractiveness of the activities for the end users of that specific area.

Several studies identify and qualify which location factors are underlying at the attractiveness of a location. The answer on the question *what is the best location* differ per organization. If the location will not suit the demand of the potential end user, the property will not be sold, rented or occupied and vice versa. Therefore, even a modern office building, which is provided with all new technologies and other high tech stuff, all in favor of the end user, is incredibly hard to sell or let when the location is incorrect. Therefore, it can be assumed that accessibility, which is part of the aspect location, is one of the most important factors due to the success of commercial real estate.

At the end it can be concluded that the accessibility has influence on the succes of a location. The accessibility affects and interpreted the property value in different ways. The accessibility does steer the price per sq. m. of an office building and can be a dealmaker or dealbreaker. Therefore, this factor will always return in all kind of researchers.

2.2.3 The Office

The third aspect named by Remøy (2010) is the office building, whereby several office characteristics are taken into account causing organizations decide to (re)locate themselves in a specific office building. Characteristics that can attract organizations are parking, reception, meeting rooms, conference rooms, fitness area, coffee corner or restaurant etc. All building facilities and characteristics together play an important role for organizations to accommodate themselves. There is a relation between vacancy and building facilities, whereby the building facilities has to fit the demands of end users (Remøy & Van der Voordt, 2014).

2.2.4 Overview

After analyzing the commercial real estate market and which features are important in regarding to the success of real estate, it can be assumed that many factors drive companies to (re)locate themselves. Besides the three main aspects as described above are economic factors, political factors, the lack of local knowledge and technology important factors which determine the success of a location and its real estate.

Nonetheless, building facilities and accessibility play an important role as well with regards to the popularity of an office building or the location. Therefore, the direct vicinity, the environment or the agglomeration play an import key role in the decision of organizations of where to accommodate themselves (Dunning & Norman, 1987; Head, Ries & Swenson, 1995; Greenhalgh 2008).

Different kind of accommodation trends and conditions are important characteristics for the success of commercial real estate. One of these trends is the movement of organizations from city edges to inner city office locations (Jones Lang LaSalle, 2017). These trends are not only provided by office users (or 'the market'), but also provided by property owners. Property owners are partly responsible for the trends in the commercial real estate market (Miller, 2014). The trends and conditions are changing over time and influence the future demand along with property values. Figure 3 summarizes all three correlated aspects which do have influence on the value of a property.

Figure 3: Characteristics which influence the price

Source: Own figure

In the urban economics is location choice a frequently discussed topic and these discussions can be divided in a descriptive or normative way. The descriptive way is devoted to the explaining value of a property at a given location and the normative way addresses the issue of optimal location conditional to a given set of constrains (Debrezion, Pels & Rietveld, 2007). This research will especially address studies of the former form and therefore focus on the relation between the proximity of railway stations and property values. Nonetheless, proximity is still a fuzzy concept.

As mentioned before, there are several forms of transport, whereof transport by rail is one of them. On a daily basis, approximately over a million persons travel by train in the Netherlands and most of them are commuters and students. Accordingly, it is plausible that organizations can have major benefits when they are located nearby a railway station, instead of further away from railway stations. Not only the proximity from and to a railway station is of importance, although the size and the quality of a railway stations is relevant in relation with the demand for offices in the direct vicinity of a railway station. Hence the term railway station deserves an explanation as well in this theoretical framework.

2.3   Railway stations

In according to Zakeri, Mosavebi & Esmaeli, (2016) is there a difference between heavy railway and light railway traffic, whereby the biggest distinction is that heavy railway traffic is equal to trains and light railway traffic is equal to the streetcar or the underground. This research will make use of the same perception and so, when the term railway station is mentioned, it is related to heavy railway.

In all expectation is there a difference as well in the values and variances in both ways of public transport, because the number of consumers at heavy railway stations is higher than the number of consumers at light railway stations. In addition, heavy railway stations are scattered over the Randstad and light rail stations are only in the largest cities.

Several business sectors and companies do have interest to locate themselves at well[1] accessible locations, such as railway stations, and therefore not only the availability of a railway station matters, but also the quality of a station is of importance. De Graaff, Debrezion & Rietveld (2007) agreed with this and added the term 'RailStation Quality Index' (RSQI). This index number measures the quality of a railway station by clarifying three components:

- Size of the railway station. The size of a railway station is measured by the total number of departures of trains. This shows how important the connection with other stations is (*Oi*).

---

[1] Note that the term well is always subjective.

- The generalized travel time between the station of departure and the station of destination. This time depends of the average waiting time, the actual time travel per train, the time for transfers and a 'penalty' for the total number of transfers ($GTJij$).
- The ratio of the generalized travel time and the distance between two stations. If the distance is relative high, than it is possible that the train makes a detour and therefore, it can be attractive to make use of other forms of transportation ($\frac{GTJij}{dij}$).

The final weighting factor is the result of the following formula:

$$\ln\frac{Tij}{OiDj} = \beta \ln GTJij + \gamma\ln\frac{GTJij}{dij} + \varepsilon ij$$

Source: De Graaff, Debrezion & Rietveld (2007)

Due to the rapidly changing mobility (OV-bureau Randstad, 2011) is a railway station an increasing place where people meet each other and work. The result is that railway stations not only grow in square meters, but also grow in the number of travellers and consumers. This has consequences for the total number of departures and arrivals and thus for the value of the RSQI.

In summary, it can be concluded that not only the distance from and to the nearest railway station has influence on the value of an office building. The quality of the nearest railway station has influences on the rent level as well. On top of that, it is interesting to investigate the interaction between the distance to the nearest railway station and the quality of that station and what the effect of the interaction is on the value of an office building.

2.4 Literature review of empirical studies

The second aspect named by Remøy (2010) is location and is the most important characteristic in this research. In addition of the academic researches as mentioned in chapter 1.3.1 provides this section insights in other relevant studies, whereby the accessibility or proximity and the rent levels of offices are centralized. In contrast with dwellings, where multiple researches are done with regards to the characteristics which forms the value or price, is the empirical research of offices and other commercial real estate limited.

In this section most relevant studies with similar topics will largely be analysed in a chronological way. The purpose of this section is to evaluate which research methods are used in earlier researches and what the results are. Relevant academic studies which focus on the value of offices are among other things the empirical researches of Clapp (1980), Ryan (1997), Cervero and Duncan (2002), Nappi-Choulet (2007), Shyr and Fu (2010), Weterings et. al. (2009) and De Graaff, Debrezion and Rietveld (2007). All these researches treat components which are relevant for this study. Some authors investigate more the effect of large cities and the office rent, others focus rather on the effect of railway transportation and which effect transportation has on rent levels.

One of the first researchers who applied a hedonic pricing method to declare office values was Clapp (1980). In this research where not only the building characteristics included in the model to explain the different office values, but also the location characteristics. The three location characteristics where related to the distance from an office to the central business district, the travel time of the employee to the office and the number of square meters of available office space in the direct vicinity. The result of this research was that all three characteristics where significant and support the vision that many organisations are well willing to pay a higher rent level for office space at the central business district. In according to the research of Clapp (1980) stimulates the central business district the possibilities of face to face contact with employees of other organisations, especially in the central business district.

A few years later Ryan (1997) empathizes with his study the interest of transportation accessibility. Within this research Ryan (1997) focuses on the value (rent) of two types of commercial real estate: industrial and office properties. His database consists of 120 properties and 500 industrial properties, collected from the San Diego metropolitan region over the period 1986-1995. To test the assumption, Ryan (1997) used a multivariate regression analysis. The dependent variable in this research was the asking rent and examples of in the depending variables where among other things the straight-line distance of each property to the nearest freeway on/off ramp, the distance to the nearest light rail station and the distance to the central business district of San Diego. The result of this study was that light rail did not have a significant effect on the rent level. Despite Ryan remarks in his analyses that there is a distinction between light and heavy railway traffic, in his research he focuses exclusively on light rail transportation. The conclusion of this research is that light rail is not significant for office rents and therefore, the question arises if the accessibility by heavy railway do have significant results or not.

The thoughts of the positive relation between the land value and a light railway station is confirmed in the study of Cervero and Duncan (2002). In this study it appears that substantial capitalization benefits were found in order to the relation between a railway station and the land value. Namely, 23% for a typical commercial parcel near a light rail transit stop and more than 120% for commercial land in a business district and within 400 meter of a commuter rail station. They describe that such evidence is not only useful for developers and lenders, but also for transit agencies who are facing lawsuits over purported negative externalities associated with being located near railway stations. In the same research by Cervero and Duncan (2010) is the term commuter rail introduced. Despite they use this term separate from the term light rail, a clear understanding is not made yet in this source.

Mourouzi-Sivitanidou (2002) argues that prevailing rents do deviate from long-run levels. The empirical results of this study indicate that variation is determined by office employment factors, such as size, diversity, spatial organization, growth rates and volatility. Besides these employment factors do other characteristics have influences on the rent level of an office as well, such as the construction costs, the opportunity cost of commercial capital, the amenities of the direct environment and the regulatory government. This research betabes also that the demand of offices is shifting away from the central cities towards the suburbs. This is in contradiction with the face to face contact as mentioned by Clapp (1980) and the current trend as stated by Jones Lang LaSalle (2017).

Besides researches by Ryan (1997) and Cervero and Duncan (2002), who both took the characteristic distance to the central business district already in account, Nappi-Choulet et. al. (2007) goes further and underline the interest of this variable. In this research it has been proved that offices in the central business district do have a significant higher rent levels than other offices locations in the city. The research area in this research was the metropolitan Paris in France. Even though this result is not very surprising, it needs to be mentioned that in this research the only location characteristic was the geographical demarcation of suburbs and no other characteristics where included, such as distance to a railway station or the level of green in the direct vicinity of an office. Therefore, the central location of a suburb has the same values as locations on the edge of the same suburb.

In the prematurely balance, it is clear that the distance from and to the central business district of a city do have a positive influence on the rent level of an office, due to the fact that face to face contact is desired and the accessibility to this district is mostly good. However, most researches focus on light rail transportation, such as streetcars and undergrounds. Therefore, the impact of heavier railway is still underexposed.

Research by Andersson, Shyr and Fu (2010) provide insights in the relation between the high-speed railway line accessibility and the residential property market. Nonetheless this research focuses on the residential market of Taiwan, it is one of the few researches with the focus on high-speed rail or heavy railway accessibility. The implied price of high-speed accessibility is estimated by using hedonic pricing method and the authors Andersson Shyr and Fu conclude that the high-speed railway accessibility has a minor effect on the housing prices. Even though this research point of convergence is on the residential market of Taiwan, it is still interesting to know that not all commercial real estate has (large) benefits of high speed railway stations.

One of the most valuable and recent studies which measures the effect of the direct vicinity on real estate prices is executed by Weterings et. al. (2009). Despite that this research argues that the effect of accessibility by public transport (including railway stations) has a positive effect on the rent level of an office, is this research still a bit superficial. As it is unknown what the average effect is on the rent level of an office when the distance to the nearest railway station increases. However, this research is still appropriate, due to the fact that Weterings et. al. sets out clearly the term 'location characteristics'. This term is split into two variables: environmental characteristics and accessibility characteristics. The characteristics 'distance to the nearest railway station' and 'railway station quality' belong both to the latter group.

By the passing of time, the literature about the influence of accessibility and the value of commercial real estate is increasing. However, it still not sufficient to answer the research question of this thesis, see section 1.2. One of the most recent studies by De Graaff, Debrezion and Rietveld (2007) is most specific with regards to the topic of this thesis. Not only the influence of a railway station of an office has been investigated in this research, also the financial impact on the rent level of office buildings is discussed. This research made use of the collected data between 1983 and 2007 by the real estate consultant DTZ, whereby the total number of offices in the database is equal to 11.298. The office characteristics in this research where divided in four groups: accessibility, building, location and regional characteristics. De Graaff, Debrezion and Rietveld (2007) conclude that the value of an office will increase with approximate 16% whether this office is located within a circle of 500 meters of a Dutch railway station. However this research is quite proper, the results provide still a global story and do have a few constraints. One of them is that the results are not applicable to case-studies, whereby infrastructural improvements are made. Besides, there is a gap between the used data and the available data of more recent times.

Overall, the conclusion of this empirical research is that there are fewer researches publicized whereby the effect of a railway station (light and heavy railway traffic) is added as one the supplementary variables on the value of offices. However, researches that do include this variable in their study, argue that there is a relation between distance to the nearest railway station and the office value. Nonetheless, it is still unknown how this relation is constructed anno 2018 and what will happen when infrastructural improvements are made.

2.5   Conceptual Model

To frame and execute this research, it is important to clarify all information of this theoretical framework in one model and to clarify the research topic. Thereafter, it is clear which connections are made and which relations exist between variables. To visualize this information, a conceptual model will be formed.

This thesis focus on the relation between the proximity to a railway station and the rent level of an office. As argued in section 2.2 the rent level is constructed by several aspects. First of all the (regional) economy influences the real estate market performances, including the employment opportunities and the success of organizations. Furthermore is mentioned that the attractiveness of an office (location) finds his origin in the proximity of multiple amenities among other railway stations. On top of that is mentioned that end users prefer offices that have great accessibility and people in general are well willing to pay for characteristics when the product satisfied the consumer (Homburg, Koschate and Hoyer, 2005). This suggest the thoughts that there is most likely a relation between railway stations that are well accessible and the rent level of offices in the direct vicinity. If applicable, it is plausible that the rent level per sq. m. will be higher, whether the distance to a railway station will be reduced. The third aspect are the office characteristics self. The rent level per sq. m. will be higher when these office characteristics will satisfy the potential tenants and will be lower when these office characteristics do not meet the requirements of end users. Figure 4 visualise this in a conceptual model:

Figure 4: Conceptual model. Step 1

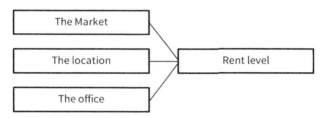

Source: Own figure

As mentioned, this research focuses on the distance of a railway station in relation with the value of an office. By studying the literature, it can be concluded that there is a strong relation between location and the accessibility. As explained in section 1.2 there is a difference between accessibility and proximity, whereby proximity is more robust than accessibility. This research focuses on the proximity of a railway station. This has effect on the previous conceptual model and results in a new conceptual model, see figure 5. To demonstrate the focus of this thesis, the connections between the rent level on the one hand and the market and the office on the other hand are disconnected.

Figure 5: Conceptual model. Step 2

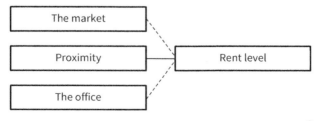

Source: Own figure

This research aims to investigate the proximity of the nearest railway station and summarizes this in the term 'distance railway station', see figure 6. By analysing the underlying data in the next chapters and define which characteristics influences the rent level of an office, it can be investigated how strong the relation is between the distance to the nearest railway station and the rent level of an office.

With the obtained knowledge, strategical (location) decisions can be made by several stakeholders. Among other things by the (local) government in regards to the (re)develop of railway station areas and what the theoretical influence is on the rent level of an office after this development. Other stakeholders are companies or organizations, so they know how the rent level of an office is constructed in relation with the distance to the nearest railway station.

Figure 6: Conceptual model. Step 3

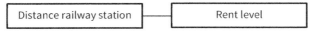

Source: Own figure

2.5   Hypotheses development

As mentioned in section 2.4, not a lot empirical research has been published in which the effect of a railway station in relation with the rent level of an office is investigated. However, through the bid rent model of Alonso (1964) conducted by of the theory by Von Thünen and more recent research by e.g. Cervero and Duncan (2002); Debrezion, Pels and Rietveld (2007); De Graaff, Debrezion and Rietveld (2007) it can be concluded that there is a relation between the rent level of an office and the distance to the nearest railway station. This results in hypothesis 1.

On top of that, it can be suggested that the quality of a railway station, expressed in the RSQI, influence the rent level. The expectation is that the RSQI positively influence the rent level of an office and this results in hypothesis 2.

The third and final hypothesis of this research suggest that the distance and RSQI has more impact on the office market in areas where the density is high, as meant in the bid rent model by Alonso (1964) and the location theory by Von Thünen (1783 – 1850), than it has in a less span office market.

Hypothesis 1

H_0:   An office which is located close by a railway station has a higher rent level per square meter lettable floor area than an office that is located further away from a railway station, whereby other relevant characteristics are taken into consideration.

H_1:   An office which is located close by a railway station has not a higher rent level per square meter lettable floor area than an office that is located further away from a railway station, whereby other relevant characteristics are taken into consideration.

Hypothesis 2

H_0:   The RSQI positively moderates the effect of distance on the rent level of an office per sq. m. LFA.

H_1:   The RSQI does not positively moderates the effect of distance on the rent level of an office per sq. m. LFA.

Hypothesis 3

H_0: In a high density and span office market is the effect of distance and the RSQI on the rent level of an office higher than in a less span office market.

H_1: In a high density and span office market is the effect of distance and the RSQI on the rent level of an office not higher to a less span office market.

The three hypotheses above are supporting to provide a satisfying answer to the research question. In the next chapter the methods of this research will be explained which will result in the most effective way to find a conclusive answer on the research question. In chapter 4 the results of the quantitative case-study will be discussed. Chapter 5 will present the answers to the hypotheses, as well as the central question.

Chapter 3   Methods

This research aims to identify the relation between the rent level of an office with regards to the distance from and to the nearest railway station. Through this identification it is the target to gather more information about the economic interest of (local) governments and the location choice of companies. Firstly, it will be clear which research method is most effective to provide a sufficient answer on the central question. Secondly, in section 3.2, the theory of the hedonic pricing method will be explained followed by the validity and the reliability of this method. The third section explains which datasets are used for this analyses and section 3.4 zooms in on the operationalization of the used dependent and independent characteristics, whereby not only the variables, although the way of how these variables are used in the statistical analysis will be explained. After the construction of the database, the outliers will be discussed, as shown in section 3.5. Finally, section 3.6 will discuss the ethics of this research.

3.1   Type of method

After the visualization of the conceptual model, it is clear which correlation will mainly be tested in this research. The data that is essential in order to execute this research, is double-sided. On the one hand consist the data of characteristics that influence the rent level of an office building and on the other hand the rent level itself. This research will be executed on behalf of a case-study to provide proper insights in the office market. The dataset need to be reliable whereby measurable data is essential and lead to the decision to execute this research in a quantitative way. One of the benefits of conducting quantitative research methods, is that more observations can be analyzed in contrast to qualitative research methods. To use proper data, the objective results show the statistical results of the office market in the Randstad.

This research does not solely use characteristics which are used in earlier studies to measure the value of an office, this study uses characteristics which have not been used before. One of the examples the grade of an office building, please see section 3.4.2. Therefore, this study make use of deductive and inductive research techniques (Verhoeven, 2014). Subsequently, a brief description will be given about the definition of this research.

What?
In order to provide a sufficient answer on the central question there are multiple office characteristics outlined that influence the rent level of an office building. These characteristics are explained in the sections 2.2, 2.3 and 2.4. Aside from these features, special attention is given to other office features, which might also have influence on the rent level of an office, only are not used in earlier researches.

Who
The population of this research are the rent levels of offices per sq. m. LFA located in the Randstad and provides insights over this geographic area by making use of a case study. The definition of the Randstad is given in section 1.3.3.

When
The database that will be used consists of all rent transactions that took place in the years 2013-2017. This period is partly dictated by years of the financial crisis and partly characterized by economic upswings. The results of this study are applicable to this time period. However, by analyzing and reflecting the results, it is possible to detect whether there is a trend or not and what can probably be happen in the near future.

Where
This research can only provide statements that are based on statistical results for offices that are located within the Randstad.

3.2   Hedonic pricing method

To determine the effect of the proximity of a railway station on the rent level of an office (location), a hedonic pricing method is the best method. This method identifies the price structure of a property and clarifies which characteristics do have influences on the value (rent level) of an office building. Due to the fact that real estate is heterogeneous, the value of real estate is structured by the value of the property plus the value of the (direct) environment. In this section the theory of the hedonic pricing method will be provided. The theory will be followed by an explanation of multiple advantages/disadvantages and reliability of this method. Subsequently, the theory of correlations will be discussed and this section will be finalized with the theoretical explanation of the multiple regression analyses, which is essential for the hedonic pricing method.

3.2.1 Theory of a hedonic pricing method

As assumed in earlier sections, this research aims to identify the relation between the value of an office and the distance to the nearest railway station. There are several methods to express these values, one of them is the hedonic pricing method, whereby the quality of the environment and the property is valued by the users of it, based on property prices or the rents. The hedonic pricing model is based on the consumption, whereby the consumption is equal to the interconnection between multiple characteristics. In other words, multiple characteristics together form the value of a consumption. Within this multiple regression, each characteristic of the consumption will have an individual value in relation to other attributes. By separating all characteristics and providing them with an individual value, it became possible to investigate the value of one characteristic within the total value. The price of one characteristic is the hedonic price or shadow price and all characteristics together, forms the price of the consumption. The most common application of the hedonic pricing method is the property market and in particular the housing market (Tyrväinen 1997; De Graaff, Debrezion & Rietveld, 2007; Waterings et. al., 2009).

The hedonic pricing method is an effective way to single out the effect from one characteristic to a number of characteristics composing a property. In the specification of the hedonic pricing method are the characteristics of an office split into two categories. On the one hand the characteristics of the office and on the other hand the characteristics of the environment.

3.2.2 Pros and cons

The hedonic pricing method has multiple advantages. First of all, the fact that the hedonic approach is founded upon a sound of economic theories and is capable of producing valid estimates of economic benefits, is that one item, of all the items that forms the total value of a product, can relatively easy be analyzed. Secondly, a lot of direct and indirect effects of the consumptions are involved in the analysis, without the need of specification of all effects, because involved characteristics can largely overlap and complement each other.

Whether one characteristic of the rent level of an office is not included in the regression, the regression shows biased results and if one characteristic is missing, the regression suffers from Omitted Variable Bias (Albert, 2018). The problem of omitted variable is reflected in misspecification of the regression model, since data is not included in the formula (due to the fact that data is not available or just forgotten to include in the database). The misspecification intends that one or more variables that are part of the regression will be over-estimated or under-estimated.

To hold omitted variable bias, two conditions in the regression analysis must hold. To begin with, the omitted variable must be correlated with the dependent variable and secondly, the omitted variable must be correlated with at least one other independent variable.

Unfortunately, the hedonic pricing method has also a few limitations. First of all, is the fact that a huge dataset is required, whereby statistical problems may hinder its feasibility. Thereby, the assumptions rely on a freely functioning of an efficient real estate market, wherein the approach only reflects the impact of the extent that individuals are aware of. On top of that, it is difficult to measure all characteristics that influence the price of the consumption in a correct way. If characteristics will be ignored or over-valued, the results are over- or underestimates as well. At the end, by making use of existing data, an ex post valuation is used on facts and is therefore not capture on non-use values (Bann, 2002).

However, the expectation is that most of the characteristics are expressed in the price of the property and thus, in the rent level (Weterings et. al., 2009 with reference to Marlet et. al., 2007 and Rodenburg 2005). Finally, it can be mentioned that this method is a bit deprecated, however it is still the most proper way to investigate one specific item that forms the value as other researches that investigate similar topics use this form of research as well. Therefore, the hedonic pricing method is the best construction to provide the following question: what is the effect of a railway station in relation with the rent level of an office?

3.2.3 Validity and reliability of the hedonic pricing method

The validity of a hedonic pricing method is mostly limited, due to the fact that there is a difference between what people argue they do and what people really do (Weterings et. al., 2009). However, the methodology has increased in the last years. For instance, by adding a factor that corrects and makes use of a limited number of alternatives, expressed in words or pictures and less susceptible for social behavior (Weterings et. al., 2009 with reference to Koopmans, 2005 and Carson, 2000).
In this study the relation is between what people argue they pay for an office per sq. m. LFA and what they really pay relieved, because the since rent level is the realized rent price per sq. m. LFA of an office. The achieved rent prices are the net prices of an office per sq. m. and thus without any form of incentives.
Furthermore, the hedonic pricing method is able to determine the relative weight of the environmental qualities in relation with other factors which influence the rent level of an office (Weterings et. al., 2009). The results are not only valid for the research unit, due to the number of cases in this research. However, in all likelihood, also valid for the entire population of offices that are located in the Randstad. As a consequence, it can be concluded that the validity of this study is high.

A reliable conclusion is only possible when the database is well-stocked. Besides the rent level (the net price that is actually paid), other characteristics must be included in the database as well, such as the characteristics of the office building and the physical, social and functional characteristics of the environment. Nonetheless, it is possible that not all characteristics can be included in the hedonic pricing method, because two (or more) characteristics influence each other in such way, that the results will be distort. This phenomenon is called the multicollinearity problem. In the subsequent section and in section 3.5.2 this issue be demonstrated and the results analyzed. However, this research is extremely reliable, since this research is based on facts (achieved rent levels) and the total number of cases is sufficient (N = 2,940).

3.2.4 Correlation

Prior to composing the hedonic pricing model, a closer look at the correlation is recommended, in order to counter multicollinearity. The correlation provides insights regarding the strength and direction of the relation between variables. The correlation can be measured with the 'Pearson correlation coefficient' (R), whereby the results differ between -1 and 1. If there is a full correlation between two variables, the result will be -1 or 1. If there is no correlation at all, the result will be equal to 0.

There is a supposed theoretical relation between the dependent variable and the independent variables. When investigating the relation between these two variables, it will be clear that there is not only a theoretical relation, but there is a statistic relation as well. When multicollinearity takes place, the relation between variables is larger than 0.9 (Baggen, 2011 with reference to Field, 2005 and De Vocht, 2007). If such a strong correlation is found, one of the variables will not be adapted in the hedonic pricing method. Which variable this is, depends on the explanatory value. The correlations will be used to complete the hedonic pricing method.

Another way to verify whether variables correlate with each other is through the variance inflation factors (VIF). When the VIF result exceeds the value of 10, multicollinearity appears. A VIF that is closer to zero, means a better outcome (Kumari, 2008). In case the correlation coefficient or the VIF value is higher than described above, one of the correlated independent variables should be removed from the dataset. In this research is the VIF will be calculated and analysed in section 3.5.2.

3.2.5 Multiple regression

In a hedonic pricing method is a consumption considered as a combination of multiple characteristics. Hence, this method will be executed by a multiple regression. This phenomenon is construct the same way as a single regression, however a multiple regression describes the relation between one dependent and multiple independent variables instead of one variable at both sides. In formula, a multiple regression can be described as:

$$Y = A + B_1 * X_1 + B_2 * X_2 + \ldots + B_i * X_i + e$$

In this study, 'Y' is equal to the rent level per sq. m. of an office and the letter 'X' represents several characteristics that form or do have influence on the price. The letter 'A' in the formula is equal to the intersection with the y-axis. Thus, the value of Y when all independent variables are equal to 0. Every independent variable has a partial regression coefficient that shows the influence of the variable at the dependent variable Y. This is corrected by the influence of other independent variables and represented with the letter B. The letter 'e' is the error-term and shows the differences between the observed value of 'Y' and the, by the formula estimated, value. The letter 'e' has to be interpret as the inexplicable part of the regression (Weterings et. al., 2009).

The multiple regression analysis investigate the statistical relation between one dependent variable and multiple independent variables. To execute a multiple regression, a set of 6 conditions have to be clear (PBL, 2006; Baggen 2011, with reference to Des Rosiers et. al., 1999; De Vocht, 2008). These 6 conditions are:

1. The variables has to be measured at the scale of interval or ratio. Independent variables may also be categorially variables.
2. No multicollinearity is allowed. This mean that the model is not allowed to have variables that correlate with each other in a strong way, because these independent variables

influence the dependent variable in such a heavy way, that this has effect on the reliability of the model.
3. There has to be a normal distribution.
4. The residual score has to be a normal distribution (no autocorrelation).
5. Heterogeneous of the variation is not allowed.
6. Autocorrelation is not allowed.

Assumption 1 and 2 will be discussed in section 3.4.2 en 3.5.2. Assumption 3 up and including 6 are conveniently arranged in appendix 1. The conclusion of these tests is that the database meet all the requirements and the multiple regression/hedonic pricing method can be calculated.

Finally, there are two methods to execute a regression model, via the standard regression and via the stepwise regression (Van Hees, 2016). The method of the standard regression add all independent variables at once in the final regression model, with the result that also not significant variables are included in the regression model. The stepwise regression method add the independent variables to the model one by one in order of their suspected effect at the dependent variable. In this method are only significant variables included in the regression model. The purpose of this method is to control the parameters per independent variable.
Both methods, standard and stepwise, do have pros and cons. In this research is chosen for the standard method, because this method is based on theoretical research while the stepwise method is mostly based on probability calculation (Van Hees, 2016 with reference to Sribney, 2011).

3.3 Dataset

The third section of this chapter will explain which datasets and characteristics are applied in this research. To examine the correlation between the distance of a railway station and the rent level of an office, a multiple regression will take place. This regression estimates the relation between the dependent variable (Y) and the independent variables (X). Whereby, based on the literature, a causal relation can be interpreted (Weterings et. al., 2009). The dependent characteristic in this thesis is the rent level per sq. m. LFA. The independent characteristics, are various characteristics that influences the rent level.

Rent level
There are two types of datasets that can be used. A dataset which provide insights in the price per sq. m. LFA of the current supply and a dataset with registered rent transactions. To provide better insights in the construction of the rent levels of office buildings, is in this research the database of JLL used, this organization is one of the largest real estate consultants worldwide.
In this dataset are the rent levels of almost 3,000 rent transactions in the Randstad conveniently arranged and expressed in sq. m. LFA.
By making use of the dataset with realized transactions, a better overview can be presented at the end of this research. As explained in section 3.2.3 is the validity of a hedonic pricing method mostly limited, due to the difference between what people argue they do and what people really do. However, by making use of the database with realized office transactions instead of the supply database is this problem solved.

Proximity
In the used database are the addresses of the offices conveniently arranged. By transforming the addresses manually into longitude and latitude data, the geographical coordination is found and can, by using the computer program GIS, be presented on a map. The same is accomplished for all

railway stations in the Randstad. Thereafter, the two separates maps can be placed on top of each other and the distance between the offices addresses and the railway stations can be measured.

RSQI

The definition railway station quality index is introduced by the researchers De Graaff, Debrezion and Rietveld (2007). Due to the fact that these researchers provides an explanation of the calculation for the index number of railway stations, it is possible to calculate the index number. However, after a personal conversation between the author of this research with dhr. T. de Graaff the dataset with the index number per railway station in the Netherlands is obtained. Despite the fact that this list is dated by 2007, the dataset is certainly functional. This can be explained by the fact that it is not relevant which railway station contains a index number (the name of a station), however the quality of a station is of highest importance in this case.

The results of this research are mean to provide an explanation of the relation between the distance from or to the nearest railway station and the rent level of an office and not to provide insights in which railway station has the highest rent level of offices in the direct vicinity.

Other

The topics above are the main valuable characteristics of this research. However, as assumed in the theoretical framework do have other characteristics influences on the rent level of an office per sq. m. as well. Most of the data is provided by JLL and includes the characteristics, surface of the transaction, grade, consultant, zip code and transaction year. Currently, almost all important characteristics that do have influence on the rent level are added to the database. In addition, the construction year of an office building as well since deprecated office buildings are less popular in comparison with old (monumental) or new office buildings. Construction year data is found from BAG, an online platform where real estate data is arranged, such as the surface of the building, intended purpose (office, retail, industrial), zip code and the construction year. The data is considered as reliable since the information on this website is provided by the Dutch chamber of commerce.

A description of what these characteristics are and why these characteristics are important with regards to the rent level will be presented in the section 3.4 operationalization. An overview of all characteristics and all related sources of it are arranged in table 1.

Table 1: Overview variables

Variable	Source
Rent level	JLL
Surface of the transaction	JLL
Construction year	Bag viewer
Grade	JLL
Consultant	JLL
Distance to the nearest railway station in meters	GIS
RSQI of the nearest railway station	Thomas de Graaff
Zip code area	JLL
Transaction year	JLL

Source: own table

Spatial fixed effects vs. random effects

Spatial fixed effects can be divided in two forms, first of all fixed effects and secondly random effects. The standard reasoning behind this, is that those effects control for all space specific and time invariant characteristics whose omission could bias the estimates in a cross-sectional study (Elhorst, 2017 with reference to Baltagi, 2005). In the fixed effects is for each spatial unit a dummy variable introduced, while in the random effects a random variable is independently and identically distributed with zero mean and variance. By creating dummy characteristics and comparing these dummies with their reference category, changes over time are included in the database. These spatial fixed effects occur Omitted Variable Bias (see section 3.2.2).

The space specific and time invariant characteristics of this research are the zip code and transaction year. By including the zip code of an office in the database, information about the geographical area is provided, along with information regarding the direct environment. This research assumes that all characteristics that do have influence on the environment are involved in the hedonic pricing model such as green facilities, the distance to the exit roads or other mobility characteristics, the distance to other facilities and forms of regional and economical characteristics and so on. By implementing the characteristic transaction year, changes over time within the zip code area are monitored and involved in the database. Whereas by including the zip code, an overview on national or regional scale and a comparison between these elements can be presented.

3.4   Operationalization

This section shows how all characteristics, that will be used in the hedonic pricing model, are operationalized. All characteristics are filtered by the used datasets or manually added, see previous section.

In order to execute the multiple regression in the right manner it is crucial that the variables are measured on interval or ratio scale. Not all variables do directly meet this criteria, since these variables are categorized for example and need therefore to be converted into dummy variables.

As assumed, consist the formula of the multiple regression of one Y characteristic and multiple X characteristics. The letter Y in this research reflects the rent level of the transaction per sq. m. LFA and the letter X reflects all characteristics that influences the rent level. By adding the dependent and independent variables, several regressions and other statistical tests can be executed. All these different independent characteristics will be introduced in this section, including a short explanation/definition of each characteristic. However, in order to be through, the dependent Y variable will be explained first in section 3.4.1.

3.4.1 Dependent variable

Y = Rent level of the transaction.

The dependent variable in this research is the value of an office expressed in the rent level per sq. m. LFA per year. Due to the fact that real estate is heterogeneous, the price per sq. m. is the only standard to compare real estate with each other. In the obtained value of office transactions no allowance is made for any form of incentives.

The rent level is measured on a scale ratio and the average rent level is € 157.14 per sq. m. LFA with a standard deviation of € 69.29. Next chapter, section 4.1, will elaborate on the variations of the rent levels.

3.4.2 Independent variables

This section will discuss the operationalization of the independent variables which has influence on the dependent variable an arbitrary sequence. Within the different types of characteristics a difference in the level of measuring exist. Some characteristics entail office building characteristics, whereas variables concern location characteristics and finally, the last group of the variables can be classified as market characteristics.

$X1$ = Surface of the transaction in sq. m. lettable floor area.

The used dataset solely provides only insight in office transactions with a surface that is equal or larger than 200 sq. m. LFA because smaller transactions are not frequently monitored by the consultant JLL, the provider of the dataset with rent transactions in this research.

The surface of the transaction does have influence on the rent level of an office, because larger self-contained space is mostly advantageous for the potential tenant and results in a lower rent price per sq. m. LFA. This phenomenon applies as well to offices with larger surface areas, the level of measuring is equal ratio scale.

$X2$ = Construction year of the building.

All offices that are included in the database are linked to BAG to capture the construction year. As explained in section 3.3, BAG concerns a Dutch website where office data is arranged, among other things with the construction year. The construction year is normally measured on a ratio scale, however in this research is chosen to categorize the construction year in four groups, first of all construction years before 1905, secondly construction years between 1906-1945, thirdly construction years between 1945-2000 and finally construction years subsequently to the year 2001.

By categorizing the construction year, the data is converted to an interval scale.

$X3$ = Grade.

The grade is a label number, whereby the ranking differs between an A-label, B-label or C-label. The highest ranking which an office building can achieve, is label A and this stands for a promising office building. In contrast, label C is the opposite and stands for a disadvantaged office building. Label B can be regarded as the moderate label and is a combination of both label A and label C.

The ranking of an office building is executed by the international consultants only and every property is individually ranked based on multiple office characteristics. Since the consultants simply do not rank the office buildings according to an universal checklist with clear instructions, the grade can be regarded as an abstract term. The grade depends among other things on building quality. Examples of building quality are building facilities which includes, technology, energy performance label and opportunities for development into another function. Unfortunately are not all office buildings in the database ranked with a label and in section 4.1 is the reason for this discussed. The office buildings which are not ranked are labeled as 'grade not available'. By categorizing the grade, the data is converted from an ordinal scale into an interval scale.

$X4$ = Consultant.

The real estate consultant is a representative form a real estate consultancy organization, assigned with the task to execute the rent transaction on behalf of the landlord.

The consultant is added to the database, to control whether there is a difference between the different real estate consultants in the Netherlands. A distorted overview can be the result of one consultant who is responsible for many transactions in a specific geographical area. The following consultants are included in this research, such as Cushman & Wakefield (including DTZ), CBRE, Colliers, Dynamis, JLL, Savills and VGM. In addition, there are also transactions included in the database where none of the consultants above are involved, since the transactions are executed by local real estate consultants and are summarized by the name 'PNL' (Property NL). All names of the consultants are at a nominal scale. By converting them into categories, the scale of measurement is changed from a nominal scale into an interval scale.

X5 = Distance to the nearest railway station in meters.

As conducted by the conceptual model, the most important independent variable in this research concerns the distance to the nearest railway station in meters, measured from the address of an office building to the railway station (as known as the address). The calculation of distance is conducted by computer programmer GIS. The distance is measured on a scale ratio and categorized as follows, first of all distance <100 meters, secondly distance 101-300 meters, thirdly distance 301-500 meters, fourthly distance 501-700 meters, fifthly distance 701-900 meters and finally distance >901 meters. Despite the fact that these characteristics are categorized, the distance to the nearest railway station in meters is measured on a scale ratio. In figure 8, see page 36, all railway stations and offices concern addresses which are incorporated in the database and conveniently arranged. Figure 9 shows the average distance from and to the nearest railway station per municipality in the Randstad.

X6 = RSQI of the nearest railway station.

In the database, every office address is linked to the RSQI number which is related to the nearest railway station. The railway station quality index number of all railway stations in the Randstad shows values between 0.15 and 1.46, whereby the average is equal to 0.79 and the standard deviation is equal to 0.31. This mean that the RSQI is measured on a ratio scale.

Despite the fact that the name of a railway station is not of importance with regards to measuring the relation between the rent level and the quality, the railway stations in the Randstad and their index number are arranged in appendix 2.

X7 = Zip code area.

By including the zip code area of office buildings, all effects of the environment are included and equal for the entire zip code area. Examples of these effects are regional economic factors or the number of green facilities, the average distance to other facilities, the average distance to the exit roads etc. In order to corporate the zip code and multiple transaction years, see next independent variable, the changes over time in space specific and time invariant characteristic are included in the database. As argued in section 3.3 this is called spatial fixed effects. Within the Randstad, numerous locations are eligible for comparison among each other and can therefore, correlate. To prevent this, the fixed effects are included ate the 4-digit zip code area.

X8 = Transaction year.

The data that is used in this analysis cover the rent transactions of offices within the Randstad for a period of five years, from 2013 up to and including 2017. This time slot includes years of the financial crisis and years with economic upswing. Especially at the beginning of the database, 2013-2015, the economic situation was fairly weak. During the financial crisis, the rent levels have decreased and following the year 2016 an increasing in rent levels was clearly visible (Jones Lang LaSalle, 2017). By adding the transaction year in the database, is each transaction automatically corrected for economic occurrences, such as the economic situation, (political) policy and so on. As assumed is this called spatial fixed effects, see section 3.3. Finally, the transaction year is measured on an scale interval.

As described in the introduction of chapter 2, Remøy (2010) emphasized that three aspects influences the price of a property, the market, the location characteristics and the building characteristics. All those aspects are reflected in the independent variables as mentioned above. Variable X1 up to and including variable X3 entail building characteristics while variable X4 and variable X8 are market characteristic. Finally, the variables X5 up to and including and X7 comprise of location aspects.

Figure 8: Railway station locations and office addresses in the Randstad

Legend
Dot: Office address
Star: Railway

Source: Own figure

Figure 9: Mean distance in km to nearest railway station in the Randstad, 2015

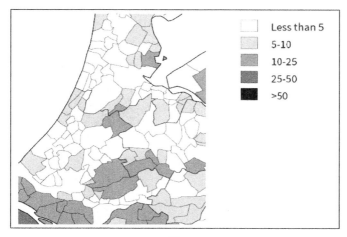

Source: CBS, April 2016

3.5   Constructing the database

This section describes the choices that are made when constructing the database for this research. Along with the data analysis, it became clear that not all values of the characteristics can be included in the regression model, which variables these are, will be explained in section 3.5.1. In section 3.5.2 is the correlation between all independent variables the central point of discussion and thereafter will an explanation of the reference categories be given. Finally, this section will ends with a brief explanation on the ethics of this research.

3.5.1 Outliers

To achieve the most desired result, it is important to have a well-structured database that is filled with office transactions. The total number of relevant office transactions is equal to the number of 2,940. Even though the database is provided by a reputable consultant and complemented by multiple prestigious organizations, it is necessary to test the database on outliers prior to the execution of the final hedonic method. In appendix 1, test 3 - second figure, is shown that there are multiple 'extreme' observations at the top tier of the rent. The highest rent level of the transactions that is included in this database is € 485.00 per sq. m. LFA. This transaction is registered in 2017 and is located in Amsterdam Zuid. Despite the fact that this rent level is high, the price is most likely accurate since this location is known as the most expensive office area in the Netherlands and rent levels above € 400.00 per sq. m. LFA are (easily) made. Thus, in conclusion, the rent of € 485.00 per sq. m. LFA is a realistic price and is therefore included in the database.

Even though there are no outliers observed at the underside of the database, is this not completely accurate. Before analysing, the rent levels lower than €50.00 per sq. m. LFA where deleted from the database. Main reason to do this, is because of the fact that this rent level is not representative for the office market in cities in the Randstad. Therefore, it can be assumed that transactions with a rent level lower than € 50.00 per sq. m. LFA are covered by registration errors. By deleting the transactions with a rent level lower than €50.00 per sq. m. LFA the validity and reliability is increased. At last but not least are the observations of the rent levels distributed as normal, see appendix 1, test 3, first figure.

3.5.2 Multicollinearity

Prior to the hedonic pricing model is it important to control the database on multicollinearity, see 3.2.4 and section 3.2.5. Multicollinearity take place when two independent variables correlate with each other in a strong way. The main reason when multicollinearity take place, is that both independent variables measures the same feature. In according to Baggen (2011 with reference to Field, 2005 and De Vocht, 2007) may the correlation, expressed in the VIF value, not be larger than 10. By analysing the VIF values it can successful be concluded that no strong correlations are found in the regression model. Unfortunately it is impossible to visualize the entire model, since the hedonic pricing method is too large when all zip codes are included as well. To make it legible, the hedonic pricing model is minimalized to 2 pages, see chapter 4.2.

By analysing the results of the hedonic pricing method and in particular the results of the VIF values is stand outs that the largest VIF value is equal to 8.884 and belong to the variable RSQI. It is unclear which variable correlate with the RSQI, however the VIF value is under 10 and is therefore still included in further analysis. All other variables that are included in the hedonic pricing method shows a VIF that differ between 1,0 and 3,0.

3.6   Ethics

The database that is used to execute the hedonic pricing method will not be published, since rent prices of office users are not registered in (semi) public documents and consist of sensitive tenant information and. Previous and current tenants of office buildings that did or do have their office in the Randstad can suffer a major loss when their financial conditions are public with regards to their accommodation.
This is in contrast with purchase prices of dwellings which are published in the chamber of commerce.

Chapter 4   Results

This chapter will explain the results of the different hedonic pricing models which will be executed to provide sufficient answers with regard to the central question and hypotheses of this research. As assumed earlier, this analysis will be executed on behalf of a case-study, whereby the research area is equal to the geographical area of the Randstad and the included railway stations are NS railway stations. This chapter starts with some fundamental descriptive statistics of the database, thereafter the hedonic pricing models will be shown and the most notable results discussed.

4.1   Descriptive statistics

Table 4 shows the fundamental descriptive statistics of the independent variables which are included in this research. By analysing these outcomes, a few remarks need to be made. The first remark is that the Valid N (listwise) shows a number of 2,736, due the fact that 204 office buildings are not registered with a construction year. When a closer look to the construction year is taken, it stands out that the minimum construction year is 1005. Unfortunately this is unrealistic and therefore it can be assumed that this construction year is dedicated to a registration error. In all likelihood the correct transaction year is 2005 instead of 1005. Despite the missing and sometimes lacking values, the expectation is that those results shows no (significant) effect on further analysis. The total number of observations is equal to 2,940 (N = 2,940).

The second aspect that stands out is the high standard deviation at the surface area in sq. m. LFA in relation with the mean of the surface. The high standard deviation is due to a few large office transactions, whereas small office transactions (<200 sq. m. LFA) are not included in the database. Nevertheless, the large transactions took place between 2013 and 2017 and to provide the most reliable results these transactions are included in the transaction database. Therefore, the mean size of a transaction is equal to 930.64 sq. m. LFA.

The third and final remark which stands out is the most important one with regard to this research and provides insights in the descriptive statistics of the distance to the nearest railway station in meters. The office which is located closest to the railway station is just at a distance of 21 meters. The office which is located most far away from a railway station is over 12 km. This office is probably located in the Southeast South-Holland, see section 3.3, figure 9.

Table 4: Descriptive statistics

	N	Minimum	Maximum	Mean	Std. Deviation
Rent per sq. m.	2,940	€ 50	€ 485	€ 157.14	€ 69.291
Surface in sq. m. LFA	2,940	200	35,701	930.64	1,690.482
Construction year	2,736	1005	2016	1954.49	139.143
Distance to nearest railway station	2,940	21	12,108	1536.96	1,354.258
RSQI	2,940	.15	1.46	.7915	.31453
Valid N (listwise)	2,736				

Source: Own table

As possibly recognized, not all variables are included in the table above of the descriptive statistics. The variables Grade, Consultant and Transaction year are not included, since these variables are officially *string* variables and therefore hard to analyse in a descriptive way. Nonetheless, analysing is possible by using the option frequencies. The frequencies of these variables are explained below, see table 5.

By analysing the tables, it stands out that over 50% of the office buildings do not have a grade (N = 1,566). Nonetheless, as assumed in section 3.4.1, are those office buildings ranked by the author as 'grade n.a.'. There are two reasons conceivable why the result of 'grade n.a.' is relatively high. The most probable reason could be that only larger consultants frequently rank the office buildings. To control this statement, the frequency of grade is calculated for the consultant PNL in the second table. As argued in section 3.4.1 is PNL a collective name for all consultants others than the largest seven. The results show that PNL does not rank the office buildings frequently, of the total not ranked offices (1,566) the largest part is due to PNL (1,447). Nonetheless, whether a closer look is taken to the first table and the offices grade n.a. (1,566) are not taken into account, approximately 25% of all office transactions are related to grade B (756).

The third and fourth table show respectively the frequency of transactions per consultant and the frequency of the total number of office transactions per year. This proves that the transactions are divided proportionally.

Table 5: Frequencies

Grade – All consultants

		Frequency	Percent	Valid Percent	Cumulative Percent
	n.a.	1,566	53.3	53.3	53.3
	A	525	17.9	17.9	71.1
Valid	B	756	25.7	25.7	96.8
	C	93	3.2	3.2	100.0
	Total	2940	100.0	100.0	

Grade - PNL

		Frequency	Percent	Valid Percent	Cumulative Percent
	n.a	1447	61.3	61.3	61.3
	A	330	14.0	14.0	75.2
Valid	B	509	21.5	21.5	96.8
	C	76	3.2	3.2	100.0
	Total	2362	100.0	100.0	

Consultant

		Frequency	Percent	Valid Percent	Cumulative Percent
	C&W	113	3.8	3.8	3.8
	CBRE	98	3.3	3.3	7.2
	Colliers	24	.8	.8	8.0
	Dynamis	29	1.0	1.0	9.0
Valid	JLL	221	7.5	7.5	16.5
	PNL	2362	80.3	80.3	96.8
	Savills	19	.6	.6	97.5
	VGM	74	2.5	2.5	100.0
	Total	2940	100.0	100.0	

		Frequency	Percent	Valid Percent	Cumulative Percent
				Year	
Valid	2013	478	16.3	16.3	16.3
	2014	590	20.1	20.1	36.3
	2015	661	22.5	22.5	58.8
	2016	560	19.0	19.0	77.9
	2017	651	22.1	22.1	100.0
	Total	2,940	100.0	100.0	

Source: Own table

In figure 10 the descriptive statistic of the average rent level and number of office transactions is visualized in a clustering of multiple zip codes and summarized as a corop. A corop is a demographic area that includes multiple cities and villages and their region. In appendix 3 are the descriptive statistics of the price per sq. m. LFA per corop region arranged in a table.

Figure 10: Average rent prices per corop and number of transactions

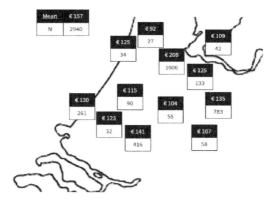

Source: Own table

The mean rent in the Randstad over the years 2013-2017 is equal to € 157.14 per sq. m. LFA. The highest average rent level per sq. m. LFA is equal to € 207.89 and is retrievable in the corop 'Groot-Amsterdam'. In all probability this is due to the office district 'Amsterdam Zuid-As', this area is considered as the best financial work environment of the Netherlands where many office transactions took place over the last years (Dynamis, 2018). The lowest average rent per sq. m. LFA is in the corop 'Zaanstreek' and is equal to € 92.26. However, only 27 transactions took place in this area. The standard deviation of the rent price per sq. m. LFA in Randstad is € 69.29 and therefore 68% of all office transactions are within a price range of € 87.85 and € 226.43 per sq. m. LFA.

4.2   The hedonic pricing model

In the previous section are the dependent and independent variables arranged in the descriptive statics. As assumed most variables are conducted by the theory and other variables, such as grade, are new research items. On behalf of a case-study in this section, it will be clarified how strong the relation is between the dependent variable and the multiple independent variables.

43

4.2.1 Various hedonic pricing models

This research especially focuses on the relation between the distance to the nearest railway station and the value of an office expressed in the rent level, whereby the quality of a railway station is of importance as well. To measure and control the effect of adding the most interesting variables and to provide sufficient answers on the central question as well as on the hypotheses mentioned in section 2.5, different hedonic pricing models are drawn, namely:

1. All variables – distance to the nearest railway station - RSQI
2. All variables + distance to the nearest railway station – RSQI
3. All variables + distance to the nearest railway station + RSQI
4. All variables + distance to the nearest railway station + RSQI + interaction

To provide an answer on the third hypothesis, a distinction between regions has to be made. The corop 'Groot-Amsterdam' will be used for the high density and span office market and the corop 'Groot-Rijnmond' will be used for the less span office market. To conduct useful results, the following two models will be developed and tested:

5. All variables + distance to the nearest railway station + RSQI, whereby transactions in the corop 'Groot-Amsterdam' are selected
6. All variables + distance to the nearest railway station + RSQI, whereby transactions in the corop 'Groot-Rijnmond' are selected

4.2.2 Interpretation of the results

Table 6 presents per column the main results of all models as described above. Only the dependent variable Y is recoded into a log variable and the results can therefore be interpreted as percentages. All independent variables can be interpreted in their original value and are compared with their reference category.

For the variables Grade, Consultant and Distance the reference category is, the category that is most frequent in the database. This means that respectively 'grade n.a.', 'PNL' and 'Distance >901 meters' are the reference categories. However, for the variables construction year, zip code and transaction year not the most frequent variables are chosen to be the reference category, but the categories 'Construction year > 2001', 'zip code 1101' and '2013' are chosen.

The main reason to choose for 'Construction year > 2001' is, because it is interesting to investigate what the impact is of new real estate developments in the direct vicinity of railway stations in relation with the rent level of an office in comparison with older office buildings. Therefore, 'new' office buildings are the reference category. As reference category for the zip code area zip code 1101 is chosen. Even though, this zip code is randomly selected, a few preferences where made. First of all, the reference category has to be reprehensive for the variable and since most office transactions of the database are registered in the city of Amsterdam, it is wise to have the reference category in Amsterdam. Second, as explained in the previous section the average rent is € 157.14 and it is recommended to have a reference category with a similar average price level. Thereafter, the average RSQI code is taken into account. However, this made no difference and thus, after the first two selections, the zip code 1101 is selected. This zip code represents various rent levels (between € 54,- and € 335,- per sq. m. LFA).

The final reference category is for the variable transaction year. To investigate whether there is a trend or not in the rent levels and the distance to a railway station and the quality of a railway station the reference category for transaction year is the oldest year in the database and therefore equals to 2013.

Table 6: Hedonic pricing model

Y = rent level in sq. m. LFA	1	2	3
Surface in sq. m. LFA	,000 (,000)	,000 * (,000)	,000 (,000)
Construction year <1905	-0,35 (,022)	-,026 (,022)	-,027 * (,022)
Construction year 1906-1945	-0,56 ** (,026)	-,041 (,026)	-,040 (,026)
Construction year 1946-2000	-0,95 *** (,013)	-,095 *** (,013)	-,095 *** (,013)
Grade A	,192 *** (,017)	,182 *** (,016)	,180 *** (,016)
Grade B	,042 *** (,014)	,044 *** (,013)	,044 *** (,013)
Grade C	-,182 *** (,013)	-,168 *** (,030)	-,174 *** (,030)
C&W	,010 (,026)	,009 ** (,026)	,010 (,026)
CBRE	,067 ** (,028)	,065 (,028)	,067 ** (,028)
Colliers	,035 (,054)	,051 (,053)	,050 (,053)
Dynamis	-,021 (,054)	-,023 (,054)	-,018 (,054)
JLL	,040 ** (,019)	,035 * (,019)	,034 * (,019)
Savills	,093 (,059)	,097 * (,058)	,094 (,058)
VGM	,025 (,031)	,023 (,031)	,023 (,031)
Distance <100		,266 *** (,044)	,263 *** (,044)
Distance 101-300		,118 *** (,023)	,115 *** (,023)
Distance 301-500		,133 *** (,022)	,129 *** (,022)
Distance 501-700		,046 ** (,021)	,047 ** (,021)
Distance 701-900		,021 (,021)	,021 (,021)
RSQI			,157 *** (,042)
Interaction <100			
Interaction 101-300			
Interaction 301-500			
Interaction 501-700			
Interaction 701-900			
2014	,069 *** (,017)	,070 *** (,017)	,072 *** (,017)
2015	,039 ** (,016)	,038 ** (,026)	,037 ** (,016)
2016	-,045 *** (,017)	-,039 ** (,017)	-,038 ** (,016)
2017	-,002 (,017)	-,001 (,016)	-,001 (,016)
Fixed effects	Yes	Yes	Yes
Constant	5,105 *** (0,30)	5,047 *** (,033)	4,958 *** (,041)
Observations	2,940	2,940	2,940
Adjusted R Square	,657	,666	,668

Notes: *p<0.1; **p<0.05; ***p<0.01 & robust standard errors in parentheses.

Table will continue at the next page.

Continuation of table 6.

Y = rent level in sq. m. LFA	4	5	6
Surface in sq. m. LFA	,000 * (,000)	4,346E-006 (,000)	,000 (,000)
Construction year <1905	-,027 (,022)	-,041 (,030)	-,035 (,069)
Construction year 1906-1945	-,040 (,026)	-,034 (,036)	-,052 (-0,,083)
Construction year 1946-2000	-,095 *** (,013)	-,094 *** (,021)	-,066 * (,036)
Grade A	,181 *** (,016)	,207 *** (,024)	,255 *** (,046)
Grade B	,044 *** (,013)	,051 ** (,020)	,078 ** (,040)
Grade C	-,173 *** (,030)	-,196 *** (,049)	-,238 *** (,072)
C&W	,009 (,026)	,022 (,032)	-,055 (,078)
CBRE	,067 ** (,028)	,044 (,038)	,071 (,075)
Colliers	,050 (,053)	,059 (,067)	,082 (,163)
Dynamis	-,018 (,054)		-,210 (,143)
JLL	,032 * (,019)	,003 (,029)	,117 ** (,046)
Savills	,092 (,058)	,135 ** (,066)	
VGM	,023 (,031)	,085 (,052)	-,097 (,081)
Distance <100	,076 (,153)	,559 *** (,088)	,190 (,116)
Distance 101-300	,123 * (,067)	,144 *** (,036)	,121 (,076)
Distance 301-500	,163 ** (,066)	,154 *** (,033)	,122 ** (,067)
Distance 501-700	,047 (,061)	-,005 (,032)	-,006 (,069)
Distance 701-900	-,018 (,059)	-,037 (,034)	,051 (,073)
RSQI	,149 *** (,044)	,369 *** (,090)	,263 * (,138)
Interaction <100	,226 (,177)		
Interaction 101-300	-,009 (,074)		
Interaction 301-500	-,039 (,072)		
Interaction 501-700	,001 (,071)		
Interaction 701-900	,048 (,066)		
2014	,072 *** (,017)	,123 *** (,026)	,115 ** (,045)
2015	,037 ** (,016)	,112 *** (,025)	,014 (,049)
2016	-,038 ** (,016)	,043 * (,026)	-,095 ** (,045)
2017	-,002 (,016)	,083 *** (,026)	-,019 (,047)
Fixed effects	Yes	Yes	Yes
Constant	4,960 *** (,045)	4,781 *** (,067)	4,746 *** (,111)
Observations	2,940	1,006	416
Adjusted R Square	,667	,672	,482

Source: Own figure

4.3   Results of the hedonic pricing model

In this section, the most interesting and outstanding results of the hedonic pricing models will be explained and discussed. By adding variables in the up following models, an interesting comparison can be made and the influence of variables on the rent price per sq. m. LFA can be explained. Although all zip codes are included in the hedonic pricing models they are not individually presented, but summarized in a text box as 'fixed effects'. The analysis includes 405 fixed-effects groups in total.

In the first model all variables are tested excluding the distance to the nearest railway station and the RSQI, this results in an adjusted R Square of ,657. The result means that approximate 65% of the rent level of an office can be explained by the variables that are included in the model. The most outstanding results are reflected in the level of grade. When an office building is labeled as a promising office building the rent level is approximately 20% higher in comparison with offices with no ranking and almost 40% higher in comparison with offices that have grade C. The difference between these labels is quite large. A possible reason for the difference could be that the office buildings with grade C or without a grade are probably office buildings that barely have any facilities and overall consist of a weak quality. Not only the building, but also the direct environment shows hardly any office benefits. On top of that all results of the variable grade are significant and therefore it can be concluded that the results are not based on coincidence.
Another notable result is that most consultants do not contribute significantly to the rent level of an office and their addition is less than 10%. This result is positive, since a consultant needs to be independent and is not allowed to create (significant) differences in the rent levels of office buildings.

In model number 2 are multiple categories in distance to the nearest railway station added to the hedonic pricing model. At first sight, this is the most interesting value of the research so far. Over 26% higher rent levels are significantly reached when an office is located within 100 meters from a railway station in comparison with an office that is located more than 901 meters away. Although the results maintain significant when the distance increases till a maximum of 700 meters, the percentage which influences the rent level decreases fast. The most likely reason to declare the decreasing level of significance (from $p<0.01$ to $p>0.1$) is that the travel time will increase when an office is located further away than 700 meters from the nearest railway station. This is due to the assumption that people probably use other means of transport, because the benefits of a railway station within walking distance disappear and other office features become more important, such as parking facilities and the level of a green environment.

In the third model all variables of this research are included in the hedonic pricing model and this results in a declared variance of approximate 67%. By including the RSQI, slightly differences can be mentioned in comparison with the previous model. However, the results of the variable distance are still significant at the level of $p<0.01$. The only considerable difference with the previous model is the addition of the railway station quality index. Nonetheless, it can be observed that the contribution of the RSQI is significant in relation to the rent level of an office building, it is still unclear what the impact of the level of RSQI really is. Therefore, figure 11 (left) visualizes the relation between the height of the RSQI and the average rent level per sq. m. LFA. After analyzing this figure, it stands out that the average rent level of an office building will decrease when a RSQI of 1.0 is reached. A plausible reason is that offices that are located in the direct vicinity of railway stations, whereby the RSQI is higher than 1.0, can hardly meet other requirements of office users. For example the parking facilities, the noise disturbance or a green work environment. The highest rent levels can statistically been reached when the RSQI of the nearest railway station is equal to 1.0.

To be comprehensive and complete, the right figure shows the relation between the rent level and the distance to the nearest railway station. This figure shows that the average rent level will decrease when the distance increases and therefore it can be concluded that the distance to the nearest railway station certainly influences the rent level of an office per sq. m. LFA. The average rent level of an office located in the Randstad, whereby the distance to the nearest railway station is equal to 200 meters, is approximately € 195.00 per sq. m. LFA. and an office whereby distance to the nearest railway station is equal to 800 meters is approximately € 140.00 per sq. m. LFA.

Figure 11: Relation of the rent level and RSQI and the relation of the rent level and distance

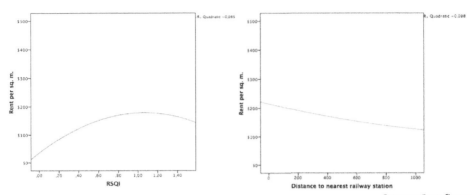

Source: Own figure

Even though the influence of the railway station quality and the influence of distance on the rent level of an office are explained, it is interesting to investigate the relation between the height of the RSQI and the distance. This relation is called the 'interaction' and is added in model 4 of table 6.

By adding the new variable interaction to the model, it stands out that in comparison with the previous model, the multiple characteristics of distance are not significant anymore. Especially the value of distance <100 shows a tremendous decrease, from over 25% with a significance level of p<0.01 to an insignificant level of 7.6%. The positive effect of distance <100 is overruled by the more robust interaction <100 effect. This implies that the railway station quality within 100 meters is more relevant than the variable distance within 100 meters.

The characteristics distance 101-300 and distance 301-500 are still significant and influence the rent level of an office positively with respectively 12.3% (p<0.1) and 16.3% (p<0.05). Therefore, it can be concluded that the RSQI positively moderates the effect of distance on the rent level of an office per sq. m. LFA. The interaction <100 shows a positive result of 22.6% in comparison with the dummy variable interaction >901, but this effect is not significant. None of the results of the interaction shows significant results. The most plausible reason for the outcome is that the quality of a railway station is more important than the variable distance. Therefore, it is more important with regards to the rent level of an office that the nearest railway station is equipped with a high quality index, instead of only the availability of a railway station. In conclusion, the effect of distance on the rent level per sq. m. LFA of an office will increase given the level of the RSQI, however, this effect is not significant. All other results of the variables are more or less the same in comparison with the previous model.

Model 5 shows the effect on the rent level in sq. m. LFA in the high density and span office market and model 6 shows the effect on the rent level in sq. m. LFA in a less span office market.

Before analysing, it is good to note that there is a relatively large difference between the number of observations between both markets. More than 1,000 observations are included in the density and span office market in comparison to 416 observations in the less span office market. To control that every category of distance is well stocked, table 7 is made. It stands out that the total number of observations in the category distance <100 do not meet the requirements to execute an statistic calculation, because N is smaller than 30, other categories should be comparable with each other. Thereafter, it stands out that not all variables have a value. The second note is that the value of the variable Dynamis is missing in model 5 and the value of the variable Savills is missing in model 6. This is the result of the fact that Dynamis was not involved in office transactions within the corop Groot-Amsterdam neither was Savills in the corop Groot-Rijnmond. The third and final note is the difference in the adjusted R Squared. In the high density and span office market the declared variance is approximate 67% and in line with previous models. The declared variance of the less span office market is approximate 48%. This means that approximately 52% of the rent level in a less span office market can be declared by variables that are not included in this hedonic pricing method.

The variable grade in model 5 and 6 shows significant results at the level $p < 0.01$. Nonetheless, the results in a high density and span office market are less positive in comparison with a less span office market. Therefore, it can be concluded that the building quality is less important in a high density and span office market than in a less span office market. This suggests that organizations are apparently less critical on the building quality of an office in a high density and span office market. Although the results in the variable distance are large, caution is necessary. In the high density and span office market the results up to 501 meters show significant outcomes. When a railway station is located within 100 meters to the nearest railway station, the rent level of an office per sq. m. LFA is 55.9% higher in comparison with an office that is located more than 901 meters away from the nearest railway station. Offices that are located within 101-500 meters from a railway station do have a significant higher rent level of approximate 15%.

In a less span office market offices nearby a railway station do have higher rent levels in comparison with offices that are located further away. However, these results are not significant. The distance 301-500 is the only significant result, it show a significant positive effect of 12.2% with $p < 0.05$. The RSQI shows in both markets a significant effect. Nonetheless, in the high density and span office market the main effect of the RSQI is 36.9% when $p < 0.01$ and in a less span office market the effect of RSQI is 26.3% when $p < 0.1$. This means that the quality of a railway station has more effect on the rent level in the corop Groot-Amsterdam than it has on the corop Groot-Rijnmond. However, in this analysis the interaction is not taken into account, because model 4 shows that the variable interaction has no significant effect.

In conclusion, organizations are less critical on the office building quality in a high density and span office market and it seems that these offices have higher rent levels per sq. m. LFA than offices in a less span office market. However, most results are not significant in the less span office market and therefore hard to compare with more significant results in the high density and span office market. In all probability the name of the location and the clustering of knowledge contributes more to the rent level of an office than the accessibility of that specific office location.

Table 7: Number of observations per category

Model 5: density and span office market (Groot-Amsterdam)		Model 6: less span office market (Groot-Rijnmond)	
Distance <100	11 observations	Distance <100	8 observations
Distance 101 – 300	93 observations	Distance 101 – 300	30 observations
Distance 301 – 500	121 observations	Distance 301 – 500	60 observations
Distance 501 – 700	111 observations	Distance 501 – 700	38 observations
Distance 701 – 901	70 observations	Distance 701 – 901	33 observations
Distance > 901	600 observations	Distance > 901	247 observations
Total	1,006 observations	Total	416 observations

Source: Own figure

Finally, it is interesting to provide insight in the trends over the past few years and to suggest a statement for the near future. Therefore, the relation between distance to the nearest railway station and transaction year is investigated and shown in table 8. By analysing this table it is clear that the declared variance (R^2) of the variable distance is increased in the last two years to nearly 9%. This means that almost 9% of the rent level will be determined by the variable distance to the nearest railway station. In comparison to earlier years this value was 6.9% in 2016, 1.7% in 2015, 2.5% in 2014 and 5.9% in 2013.

Table 8: Interaction between the rent level and distance over the years

	2013	2014	2015	2016	2017
R^2	0.059	0.025	0.017	0.069	0.086
N	478	590	661	560	651

Source: Own figure

Chapter 5   Conclusion and discussion

The final chapter of this research provides an answer on the central question and on the hypotheses of this research, whereby the results of the case-study, as executed in chapter 4, will be discussed. Furthermore, the used methodology as explained in chapter 3 will be reflected and discussed as well the recommendation for further research will be presented.

5.1   Central question and hypotheses

This research has a central question, three hypotheses and no further sub questions. In this research there are different analyses executed and is the contribution of several variables on the rent level of an office individually analyzed to provide a sufficient answer for these questions. The variables that do have influence on the rent level of an office are the construction year, the grade, the consultant that was involved in the transaction, the distance between the office and the nearest railway station, the quality of that railway station, the characteristics of the environment summarized in the zip code and finally the transaction year. These variables together result in a declared variance of approximate 67%.

This analysis focuses on the proximity of office buildings by rail, whereby theories of spatial land use and multiple office values are taken into account. The accumulation or concentration of knowledge and face to face contact are very valuable for office users in the current changing environment and therefore the research question in this research is:

"To what extent does the proximity of a railway station affect the rent of office space?"

The theoretical framework is formed by the most established location theory that is written by Von Thünen, whereby the railway stations are considered as central point. The expectation is that an office that is located close by a railway station has a higher rent level per sq. m. LFA than an office that is located further away from a railway station, whereby relevant characteristics are taken into consideration.

The results of this empirical research conclude that it is true that an office that is located close by a railway station has a higher rent level per sq. m. LFA in comparison with an office that is located further away. When the distance in proportion increases, the effect on the rent level will decrease and it can be concluded that the effect of distance on the rent level of an office building is significant until 701 meters. When the distance increases, the agglomeration benefits of the proximity of a railway station will disappear which has probably to do with the extra travel time between the office and the railway station. When an office building is located within a distance of 100 meters, the average rent level is 26.3% higher and approximate 12% higher for offices within a range of 101-500 meters from a railway station. Both characteristics in comparison with office buildings that are located more than 901 meters away from a railway station.

However, these results are too superficial, because the interaction between the distance and the quality of a railway station is not taken into account. When the interaction is added to the hedonic pricing models, it stands out that the significance level of the variables distance decreases. The interaction shows that the RSQI positively moderates the effect of distance on the rent level of an office expressed in sq. m. LFA. Though, this effect is not significant. This means that the quality is more robust than only the distance. The result is not surprisingly, because it is plausible that larger railway stations are more attractive than smaller railway stations and this is reflected in the rent level per sq. m. LFA. The quality of a railway station depends among other things on the connection with other railway stations and the generalized travel time between railway stations. The average

RSQI is 0.79 and statistically the highest rent levels of an office are reached when the nearest railway station has an RSQI of 1.0. When the RSQI is higher than 1.0, the railway station is probably so large, that other facilities which influence the rent level are scarce, such as the accessibility by car, the number of available parking places and a work environment without noise disturbance.

Despite the fact that the railway station quality is more robust than the distance, the interest of distance is slightly increasing in recent years. The contribution of distance to the rent level was 1.7% in 2015 and 8.6% in 2017.

To meet the requirements of face to face contact and global working it is plausible that as well the RSQI as the distance to the nearest railway station will progressively increase in future.

On top of this conclusion, a closer look is taken to two different types of office markets. On the one hand a high density and span office market and on the other hand a less span office market. After analysing, it can carefully be stated that organizations are less critical on the office building quality in a high density and span office market and it seems that these offices have higher rent levels per sq. m. LFA than offices in a less span office market. However, most results are not significant in the less span office market and therefore hard to compare with more significant results in the high density and span office market. In all probability the name of the location and the clustering of knowledge contributes more to the rent level of an office than the accessibility of that specific office location.

5.2   Discussion and recommendations

The quality of this research is determined by the considerations that are made during the execution of this research, whereby the most important decisions are made in chapter 3 and 4, respectively the chapter methodology and the chapter results. In this section the crucial choices and decisions will be analyzed and discussed, as well further recommendations will be presented.

Despite the fact that most decisions are made in chapter 3 and 4, a chronological start is essential for the discussion and therefore a short review will be made to chapter 2.
As mentioned is the term proximity essential for this research. To be clear and complete there has been tried to minimalize the overlap between multiple forms of accessibility, such as accessibility by rail, by road, by airplane or by water. To bring focus in this research the distance to the nearest railway station is the only variable that measures the term proximity.

In chapter 3 the methodology is explained. Besides an explanation of the method that is used to provide a sufficient answer on the central question, this chapter is focused on the collection of data. The hedonic pricing method is the best and proper way to explain the contribution of multiple variables on the value of an office, expressed in the rent level. A hedonic pricing method can only be executed when there is a lot of quantitative data available. When thinking about the research process one of the biggest challenges was to collect, filter and operationalize the available data to provide sufficient results. The available data of offices is, in contrast to dwellings, not very specific. Despite real estate is heterogeneous, dwellings always have multiple characteristics that influence the price. Besides the location and surface area the value of dwellings depend among other things on the availability of a garden or balcony and the size of it, the number of bathrooms, the size and equipment of the kitchen, the total number of bedrooms and so on. Offices do have features as well, these data is not collected in a database. These results can be more specific when details of the rent transactions are available, such as incentives, duration of the lease term, the vacancy rate after the last transaction, the number of rented parking places and so on. Nonetheless, a threat of adding to many characteristics is that multicollinearity will appear. In this research the characteristics do not overlap each other and therefore is multicollinearity not involved in the database and during the execution of the hedonic pricing method.

The hedonic pricing method is executed in chapter 4 and shows various results. Despite the fact that the results would be more specific when several office- and transaction characteristics where added to the database, the declared variance of this research is quite high, namely 66.7%. This means that approximate 33% of the rent level of office transactions cannot be declared by the variables in this model. In contrast with other comparable research by Weterings et. al. (2009), Braam (2014) and De Graaff, Debrezion and Rietveld (2007) who have a declared variance of respectively 40.5%, 47% and approximate 39% the variance of this underlying research is major. One of the reasons for this relatively high variance is due to the fact that this research take other variables into account that are never investigated before, such as grade. Another reason can be the including of zip code instead of individual variables that characterize the environment.

The results of the hedonic pricing method show clear outcomes, except the results of model 7 and model 8, when a comparison between two types of office markets is made including the interaction variable. A reason for these disturbing results is hard to declare. It is possible that the number of office transaction is not sufficient to execute a statistical analysis. However, after merging the distance categories in three groups (0-300, 301-900, >900) the results are less extraordinary, but still not significant.
Due to the fact that this research is explorative and based on quantitative input, the conclusion is informative. Therefore, the recommendations are related to the input of this research and not particularly related to the outcomes. For further research it is recommended to specify the characteristics in two ways to achieve proper results. Firstly, by adding constructive characteristics, such as energy performance label and interior characteristics and secondly, by adding details of the lease agreement and the (average) vacancy rate of the office building.

Nonetheless, the results of this research are sufficient and provide insights in the theory whether the proximity of a railway station has effect on the rent level of an office building. The results provide insights in the construction of the rent level of an office and afford organizations, tenants and office owners an extra support by the decisions in their real estate choices. On top of those stakeholders, this research is also interesting for (local) governments, due to the fact that the quality of a railway station contributes more to the value of an office than only the distance to the nearest railway station. This makes it possible for (local) governments to develop their plans and execute their policies less reactive and more proactive.

Bibliography

Albert. (2016). *Omitted Variable Bias: A Comprehensive Econometrics Review.*

Alonso, W. (1964). Location and land use.

Andersson, D. E., Shyr, O. F., & Fu, J. (2010). Does high-speed rail accessibility influence residential property prices? Hedonic estimates from southern Taiwan. Journal of Transport Geography, 18(1), 166-174.

Baggen, N. (2011). *Het effect van lightrail op de waarde van woningen in haar omgeving: Een casestudie naar het effect van de RandstadRail op de waarde van woningen in de gemeente Zoetermeer* (Master's thesis).

Ball, M. (2003). Is there an office replacement cycle? *Journal of Property Research*, 20(2),173-189.

Bann, C. (2002). An overview of valuation techniques: Advantages and limitaions.

Barkham, R., Bokhari, S., & Saiz, A. (2018). Urban Big Data: City Management and Real Estate markets.

Bijl, D. (2009). *Aan de slag met het nieuwe werken* (pp. 1-190). Zeewolde: Par CC.

Bogner, A., & Menz, W. (2008). The theory-generating expert interview: epistemological interest, forms of knowledge, interaction. In A. Bogner, B. Littig, & W. Menz, *Interviewing experts* (pp. 43-80). London: Palgrave Macmillan.

Braam, J. (2014). Een onderzoek naar de invloed van Luchthaven Schiphol op de waarde van kantoorlocaties in de Randstad. *ASRE.*

Buitelaar, E., van den Berge, M. A., van Dongen, F. A. M., Weterings, A., & van Maarsenveen, R. (2017). *De toekomst van kantoren: Een scenariostudie naar de ruimtebehoefte.* Planbureau voor de Leefomgeving (PBL).

CBS StatLine. (2018). *Regionale kerncijfers Nederland.* Centraal Bureau voor de Statistiek, Den Haag/Heerlen.

Cervero, R., & Duncan, M. (2002). Transit's value-added effects: light and commuter rail services and commercial land values. *Transportation Research Record: Journal of the Transportation Research Board*, (1805), 8-15.

Clapp, J. M. (1980). The intrametropolitan location of office activities. *Journal of Regional Science*, 20(3), 387-399.

Clapp, J. M. (1993). *Dynamics of office markets: empirical findings and research issues.* The Urban Insitute.

Creswell, J. W., & Clark, V. L. P. (2007). Designing and conducting mixed methods research.

Debrezion, G., Pels, E. A., & Rietveld, P. (2006). The impact of rail transport on real estate prices: an empirical analysis of the Dutch housing market.

De Graaff, T., Debrezion, G., & Rietveld, P. (2007). De invloed van bereikbaarheid op vastgoedwaarden van kantoren. *Antwerpen: CVS.*

Dynamis (2018). Sprekende cijfers kantorenmarkten.

de Wijs, L., Witte, P., & Geertman, S. (2016). How smart is smart? Theoretical and empirical considerations on implementing smart city objectives–a case study of Dutch railway station areas. *Innovation: The European Journal of Social Science Research, 29*(4), 424-441.

Dunning, J. H., & Norman, G. (1987). The location choice of offices of international companies. *Environment and Planning A, 19*(5), 613-631.

Elhorst, J. P. (2003). Specification and estimation of spatial panel data models. International regional science review, 26(3), 244-268.

Elhorst, J. P. (2017). *Spatial Econometrics. The basics.* University of Groningen, the Netherlands.

Enström, R., & Netzell, O. (2008). Can space syntax help us in understanding the intraurban office rent pattern? Accessibility and rents in downtown Stockholm. *The Journal of Real Estate Finance and Economics, 36*(3), 289-305.

Geltner, D. M., Clayton J., Miller, N.G., Eichholtz, P. (2014). Commercial Real Estate. *Analysis and Investments. Chapter 2,* 24-38.

Gotham, K. F. (2006). The secondary circuit of capital reconsidered: globalization and the US real estate sector. *American Journal of Sociology, 112*(1), 231-275.

Geurs, K. T. (2014). *Dynamiek in mobiliteit en bereikbaarheid.* University of Twente.

Gregory, R., Lombard, J. R., & Seifert, B. (2005). Impact of headquarters relocation on the operating performance of the firm. *Economic Development Quarterly, 19*(3), 260-270.

Debrezion, G., Pels, E., & Rietveld, P. (2007). The impact of railway stations on residential and commercial property value: a meta-analysis. *The Journal of Real Estate Finance and Economics, 35*(2), 161-180.

Galgóczi, B., Keune, M., & Watt, A. (2006). Relocation: concepts, facts and policy challenges. *Transfer: European Review of Labour and Research, 12*(4), 499-520.

Greenhalgh, P. (2008). An examination of business occupier relocation decision making: Distinguishing small and large firm behaviour. Journal of Property Research, 25(2), 107-126.

Haartsen, T., & Venhorst, V. (2010). Planning for decline: anticipating on population decline in the Netherlands. *Tijdschrift voor economische en sociale geografie,* 101(2), 218-227.

Head, K., Ries, J., & Swenson, D. (1995). Agglomeration benefits and location choice: Evidence from Japanese manufacturing investments in the United States. *Journal of international economics, 38*(3-4), 223-247.

Hess, D. B., & Almeida, T. M. (2007). Impact of proximity to light rail rapid transit on station-area property values in Buffalo, New York. *Urban studies, 44*(5-6), 1041-1068.

Hilbers, H., & Snellen, D. (2009). Mobiliteit beïnvloeden met ruimtelijk beleid, openbaarvervoeraanbod of prijsbeleid. Doen of niet doen?. Bijdrage aan het Colloquium Vervoersplanologisch Speurwerk.

Homburg, C., Koschate, N., & Hoyer, W. D. (2005). Do satisfied customers really pay more? A study of the relationship between customer satisfaction and willingness to pay. *Journal of Marketing, 69*(2), 84-96.

Jones Lang LaSalle. (2017). *Office special - Rotterdam and The Hague Region.* Rotterdam: Jones Lang LaSalle.

Jones Lang LaSalle (2017). *Outlook Kantoren 2017.*

Jonkers, W. (2017). De economieën van Amsterdam en Rotterdam vergeleken.

Kaplan, E., & Amir, A. (1988). A fast feasibility test for relocation problems. *European Journal of Operational Research,* 35(2), 201-206.

Kok, N., Koponen, E., & Martínez-Barbosa, C. (2017). ig Data in Real Estate? From Manual Appraisal to Automated Valuation. *The Journal of Portfolio Management,* 43(6), 202-211.

Krabbenborg, L., & Daalhuizen, F. (2016). DE GEOGRAFIE VAN HET WERKEN IN NEDERLAND VERANDERT.

Kumari, S. S. (2008). Multicollinearity: Estimation and elimination. Journal of Contemporary research in Management, 3(1), 87-95.

Leszczynska, D., & Pruchnicki, E. (2017). Optimal location of a multinational corporation resulting from knowledge transfer: The general mathematical formulation. *Journal of Management Development, 36*(9), 1191-1202.

Tyrväinen, L. (1997). The amenity value of the urban forest: an application of the hedonic pricing method. Landscape and Urban planning, 37(3-4), 211-222.

Miller, G. (2014). Workplace trends in office space: implications for future office demand. *Journal of Corporate Real Estate,* 16(3), 159-181.

Mourouzi-Sivitanidou, R. (2002). Office rent processes: the case of US metropolitan markets. Real Estate Economics, 30(2), 317-344.

Nadtochy, Y., Klochko, E., Danilina, M., Gurieva, L., Bazhenov, R., & Bakharev, V. (2016). Economic factors and conditions for the transformation of the education services market in the context of globalization. *International Review of Management and Marketing,* 6(1S).

Nappi-Choulet, I., Maleyre, I., & Maury, T. P. (2007). A hedonic model of office prices in Paris and its immediate suburbs. Journal of Property Research, 24(3), 241-263.

Nitsch, H. (2006). Pricing location: a case study of the Munich office market. *Journal of Property Research, 23*(2), 93-107.

OV-bureau Randstad. (2011). *Synergie tussen OV en RO.* Utrecht: OV-bureau Randstad.

Remøy, H. (2010). *Out of office: a study on the cause of office vacancy and transformation as a means to cope and prevent.* Delft: IOS Press.

Remøy, H., & JM van der Voordt, T. (2014). Priorities in accommodating office user preferences: Impact on office users decision to stay or go. Journal of Corporate Real Estate, 16(2), 140-154.

Risselada, A., Schutjens, V., & Van Oort, F. (2013). Real Estate Determinants of Firm Relocation in Urban Residential Neighbourhoods. *Tijdschrift voor economische en sociale geografie*, 104(2), 136-158.

Ryan, S. (1997). The value of access to highways and light rail transit: evidence for industrial and office firms.

Sasaki, Y., & Box, P. (2003). Agent-based verification of von Thünen's location theory. *Journal of Artificial Societies and Social Simulation, 6*(2)..

Scholz, R., & Tietje, O. (2002). *Embedded case study methods: Integrating quantitative and qualitative knowledge.* . Sage publications.

Shimizu, C., Karato, K., & Asami, Y. (2010). Estimation of redevelopment probability using panel data: Asset bubble burst and office market in Tokyo. *Journal of Property Investment & Finance*, 28(4), 285-300.

Van Hees, H. T. A. (2016). Bereikbaarheid en de Nederlandse kantorenmarkt (Master's thesis).

Van Zon, R., MRE, S. M., van den Berg, P. E. W., & de Bue, A. M. V. (2014). *Clustering en de attractiviteit van kantoorlocaties* (Doctoral dissertation, Master thesis). Technische Universiteit Eindhoven, Eindhoven, Nederland).

Verhoeven, N. (2014). Wat is onderzoek?

Visser, P. & Van Dam, F. (2006). *De prijs van de plek. Woonomgeving en woningprijs.* Ruimtelijk planbureau, Den Haag.

Vogli, R., Kouvonen, A., Elovainio, M., & Marmot, M. (2014). Economic globalization, inequality and body mass index: a cross-national analysis of 127 countries. *Critical Public Health*, 24(1), 7-21.

Wang, F. (2003). Job proximity and accessibility for workers of various wage groups. *Urban Geography, 24*(3), 253-271.

Weterings, A., Dammers, E., Breedijk, M., Boschman, S. & Wijngaarden, P. (2009). De waarde van de kantooromgeving. Effecten van omgevingskenmerken op de huurprijzen van kantoorpanden. *Planbureau voor de Leefomgeving (PBL).*

Willigers, J., Floor, H., & van Wee, B. (2007). Accessibility indicators for location choices of offices: an application to the intraregional distributive effects of high-speed rail in the Netherlands. *Environment and planning A, 39*(9), 2086-2898.

Willigers, J., & Van Wee, B. (2011). High-speed rail and office location choices. A stated choice experiment for the Netherlands. *Journal of Transport Geography*, 19(4), 745-754.

Yin, R. (2013). *Case study research: Design and methods.* Sage publications.

Zakeri, J. A., Mosayebi, S. A., & Esmaeili, M. (2016). Numerical and field investigations of track dynamic behavior caused by light and heavy railway vehicles. Journal of Theoretical and Applied Mechanics, 54(3), 871-879.

Appendix

Appendix 1 - The six requirements for the execution of a multiple regression

This appendix will discuss the requirements for the execution of a multiple regression. The SPSS results are conducted by the author.
The requirements are:

1. Variables has to be measured at the scale of interval or ratio. Independent variables may also be categorially, is so, than are these variables the dummy variables.
   See section 3.4.2

2. No multicollinearity is allowed. This mean that the model is not allowed to have variables which correlate each other in a strong way. Because these independent variables influence the dependent variable in such a heavy way, that this has effect on the reliability of the model.
   See section 3.5.2

3. There has to be a normal distribution.

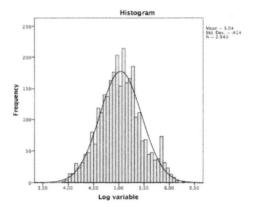

4. The residual score has to be a normal distribution (no autocorrelation).

Levene's Test of Equality of Error Variances[a]

Dependent Variable: Log variable

F	df1	df2	Sig.
1,842	2626	109	,000

Tests the null hypothesis that the error variance of the dependent variable is equal across groups.

a. Design: Intercept +
   X1Sizeofthetransaction +
   X2Building_year + X3Grade +
   X4advisor + X5Geographicalarea +
   X6Distance_nearest_railway_in_me
   ters + X7_RSQI_nw +
   X8ZIP_Code_4_numeric + Jaar

Significance level is 0,000 and suggest that the equality of variance is been satisfied.

5. Heterogeneous of the variation is not allowed.

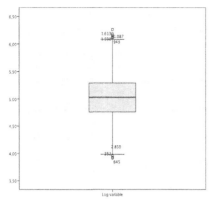

The date is homogeneous distributed.

6. Autocorrelation is not allowed.

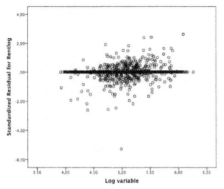

Due to the fact that the results of the analysis are random distributed up and around the 0,00 value is there no autocorrelation detected.

Appendix 2 - Railway stations in the Randstad, the Netherlands

Railway stations in the Randstad including the RSQI number					
Abcoude	0.69	Delft Zuid	0.68	Maarn	0.33
Almere Buiten	0.44	Den Haag Centraal	0.95	Maarssen	0.49
Almere Centrum	0.5	Den Haag HS	1.12	Nieuw Vennep	0.57
Almere Muziekwijk	0.49	Den Haag Laan van NOI	0.68	Nieuwerkerk a/d IJssel	0.37
Almere Oostvaarders	0.49	Den Haag Mariahoeve	0.63	Rijswijk	0.73
Almere Parkwijk	0.36	Den Haag Moerwijk	0.64	Rotterdam Alexander	0.68
Almere Poort	0.48	Den Haag Ypenburg	0.48	Rotterdam Blaak	0.64
Almere Vathorst	0.48	Diemen	0.42	Rotterdam Centraal	1.04
Alphen aan den Rijn	0.46	Diemen Zuid	0.68	Rotterdam Lombardijen	0.63
Amersfoort	0.92	Dordrecht	0.96	Rotterdam Noord	0.37
Amersfoort Schothorst	0.48	Dordrecht Stadspolders	0.25	Rotterdam Zuid	0.56
Amsterdam Amstel	0.9	Dordrecht Zuid	0.29	Schiedam Centrum	0.77
Amsterdam Bijlmer	0.58	Driebergen-Zeist	0.65	Schiphol	1.05
Amsterdam Centraal	1.06	Driehuis	0.29	Sliedrecht	0.22
Amterdam Holendrecht	0.54	Duivendrecht	1.27	Soest Zuid	0.27
Amsterdam Lelylaan	0.65	Gorinchem	0.15	Utrecht Centraal	1.46
Amsterdam Muiderpoort	0.61	Gouda	0.88	Utrecht Lunetten	0.41
Amsterdam RAI	0.6	Gouda Goverwelle	0.42	Utrecht Overvecht	0.61
Amsterdam Sloterdijk	1.06	Haarlem	0.95	Utrecht Terwijde	0.54
Amsterdam Science Park	0.49	Haarlem Spaarnwoude	0.53	Voorburg	0.52
Amsterdam Zuid	0.74	Hardinxveld-Giessendam	0.21	Voorhout	0.43
Arkel	0.08	Heemstede-Aerdenhout	0.75	Voorschoten	0.62
Baarn	0.46	Hillegom	0.49	Waddinxveen	0.21
Barendrecht	0.54	Hilversum	0.74	Waddinxveen Noord	0.22
Bilthoven	0.43	Hilversum Media Park	0.48	Woerden	0.86
Bloemendaal	0.37	Hilversum Noord	0.42	Zaandam	0.70
Bodegraven	0.42	Hilversum Sportpark	0.58	Zaandam Kogerveld	0.36
Boskoop	0.22	Hollandsche Rading	0.48	Zandvoort aan Zee	0.22
Breukelen	0.68	Hoofddorp	0.75	Zoetermeer	0.55
Bunnik	0.46	Houten	0.54	Zoetermeer Oost	0.37
Capelle Schollevaar	0.41	Leiden Centraal	1.28	Zwijndrecht	0.57
Delft	0.87	Leiden Lammenschans	0.38		

Not all railway stations of the Randstad are arranged in the table above. The missing railway stations are not linked to an office address, because other railway stations are closer by.

Source: T. De Graaf, 2007. Edited by author

Appendix 3 - Price per sq. m. LFA per corop region

Geographical area	Mean	N	Minimum	Maximum	Std. Dev.	Median
Agglomeration 's-Gravenhage	€ 130.02	261	€ 50	€ 317	€ 43.868	€ 129.00
Agglomeration Haarlem	€ 124.50	34	€ 59	€ 215	€ 38.983	€ 116.00
Agglomeration Leiden en Bollenstreek	€ 114.82	90	€ 50	€ 225	€ 35.202	€ 116.50
Delft en Westland	€ 123.19	32	€ 61	€ 159	€ 25.584	€ 130.00
Flevoland (Almere)	€ 108.57	42	€ 50	€ 190	€ 27.483	€ 107.50
Groot-Amsterdam	€ 207.89	1,006	€ 50	€ 485	€ 80.218	€ 190.00
Groot-Rijnmond	€ 140.78	416	€ 53	€ 375	€ 47.445	€ 135.00
Het Gooi en Vechtstreek	€ 124.92	133	€ 60	€ 222	€ 37.946	€ 123.00
Oost-Zuid-Holland	€ 104.41	58	€ 53	€ 201	€ 34.229	€ 101.00
Utrecht	€ 135.21	783	€ 50	€ 480	€ 43.958	€ 133.00
Zaanstreek	€ 92.26	27	€ 59	€ 141	€ 24.027	€ 85.00
Zuidoost-Zuid-Holland	€ 107.60	58	€ 50	€ 239	€ 31.056	€ 109.50
Total	€ 157.14	2,940	€ 50	€ 485	€ 69.291	€ 142.00

The visualisation is on a map is shown in chapter 4.1

Printed in Great Britain
by Amazon

83971799R00047